SONGS FOR THE SOUL

IVOR MOODY

First Published 2017 by:
Rejoice Publiscations
An imprint of Matthew James Publishing Ltd
Unit 46 Goyt Mill
Upper Hibbert Lane
Marple
SK6 7HX
www.matthewjamespublishing.com

ISBN: 978-1-910265-26-0

Printed by Gutenberg Press Ltd.

'To Ruth, Eleanor, Samuel, William and Thomas: my true colours.'

.

Acknowledgements

Scripture quotations [marked NRSV] are taken from the New Revised Standard Version Bible, Anglicized Edition, copyright © 1989, 1995 by the Division of Christian Education of the National Council of the Churches of Christ in the United States of America, and are used by permission. All rights reserved'.

THE POEMS OF GERARD MANLEY HOPKINS 4E edited by W. H. Gardner and N.H. MacKenzie (1970): 6 lines from 'Nondum' (p. 33). By permission of Oxford University Press.

Permission granted for quotation from 'Telling the Story' by Andrew Walker - London SPCK (1996) p.99

Short quote from "Exclusion & Embrace", ISBN 978067002825 by Volf, Copyright ©1996 by Abingdon Press, an imprint of The United Methodist Publishing House. Used by permission. All rights reserved.

Quote from Micheal O'Siadhail, Collected Poems (Bloodaxe Books, 2013) Reproduced with permission of Bloodaxe Books.

5 lines from 'Folk Tale' and 5 lines from 'Via Negativa' from COLLECTED POEMS 1945-1990, by RS Thomas, Reproduced with permission of Orion Books Ltd.

A GRIEF OBSERVED by C.S. Lewis copyright ©C.S. Lewis Pte. Ltd. 1961. Extract reprinted by permission. [USA rights]

C.S. Lewis, *A Grief Observed* from (London: Faber & Faber Ltd, 2013), pp.13-14. Extract reprinted by permission. [Rest of World Rights]

Foreword

Some years ago, watching a documentary about musical theatre, I remember someone commenting that for it to be truly worthwhile a song had to have a dramatic purpose; it had to have a place within the drama of the musical or opera. Thus with a dismissive flourish every pop song that has been written in the last fifty years – and for that matter a whole tradition of folk song that came before it – was consigned to the musical scrapheap.

At first I was infuriated by this snobbery. Did he really mean that Lennon and McCartney, Chuck Berry, Bob Dylan, Carole King, Joni Mitchell, Leonard Cohen, Joe Strummer, Ewan MacColl, Bob Marley and David Bowie had really written nothing of any value? Well, I fear he did; but Ivor Moody's thoughtful and penetrative book suggests something else. The commentator was half right: songs do need a dramatic purpose , a place in the drama of life, in order to have value; but with popular song that purpose will be acquired not pre-determined. The theatre in which popular song plays its part today is life itself. From the rise of pirate radio in the 1950s to Spotify and iTunes today, mass communication has enabled popular song to become the soundtrack of our lives. We think of songs as 'our songs.' We associate a song with a particular person, or moment, or emotion, or place. We invest the song with the meaning of our own lives, with all its joys and setbacks. In this sense the song really is 'my song.' It is the aria I sing – or at least listen to - for particular reasons and at particular times. Sometimes certain songs take on an even wider ownership, such as the whole crowd at Anfield, or more recently a whole city, singing and owning The Jerry and the Pacemakers hit, 'You'll never Walk Alone.' Thus the song becomes the vehicle and channel for meaning, and a place where life can be interpreted.

In his examination of the songs that have brought meaning and purpose to his life, Ivor helps us connect with the music and drama of the story of Jesus Christ, and the new song of God's loving purposes that Christians are called to sing. He interprets the songs in this way and we find new meaning in them. As he says in the Introduction: "All these songs formed a backdrop to my growing up and the discovery and exploration of my independence. Not only are they songs which I love to hear, but they all contain music and words which have struck me deeply emotionally and intellectually as songs that may contain a message for our times, and which have been important for me in the progress of my own life." These songs are a soundtrack for the spiritual life, and a connection between the longings of our culture and the faith of the Church. They are, in Ivor's words, "signposts to the spiritual."

You don't need to like the same songs as Ivor to like this book. Its themes and melodies and rhythm will resonate with the beat of your own heart.

The Rt Revd Stephen Cottrell
Bishop of Chelmsford

The Songs

Don't Let Me Be Misunderstood
Sung by Nina Simone
Written by Bennie Benjamin,
Gloria Caldwell and Sol Marcus.

True Colours
Sung by Eva Cassidy
Written by Billy Steinberg and Tom Kelly.

Message in a Bottle
Sung by The Police
Written by Matthew Gordon.

Blowin' in the Wind
Sung by Bob Dylan
Written by Billy Sherrill and Charlie Rich.

The Sounds of Silence
Sung by Paul Simon and Art Garfunkel
Written by Paul Simon.

Let it Be
Sung by Paul McCartney
Written by John Lennon and Paul McCartney.

Contents

Introduction

'The handed-downess of things reminds us that they have a history, an embeddedness in past cultures: they are a treasury of blessings to be appropriated by every new generation. The gospel comes from the past to us as a sacred and precious deposit of faith. We do not offer the world a new doctrine, but that which we have received from the beginning.'[1]

This book is about finding the sacred nestling in the apparently secular. It seeks to do so by looking at six songs which over the years have sold countless copies - they are all 'icons' in their own right. But being thoroughly immersed in popular culture and in the consciousness of millions of people as they are, I argue they contain within them a 'treasury of blessings'. An embedded signpost to the spiritual which, if we would see it, gives us powerful potential to access the numinous and the transcendent in our lives.

It is from the milieu of comprehending that theology is not here to flee or to police popular culture, but rather to try and understand it and to rediscover faith in the very fabric of the secular, that this book emerges. My inspiration for this was given wings when, in 1996, I became Chaplain of the Chelmsford Campus of Anglia Ruskin University. For the first time in my professional life I was forced to think 'outside the box,' and required to conduct Christian ministry in the midst of a secular institution where there had been very little experience of Chaplaincy. Any 'official' faith presence was a new concept, even though the seeds of Chaplaincy on campus had already been laid by some staff members who had begun to meet and who were happy to be identified as a Christian presence. As one of the 'new' universities emerging from its previous status as a Polytechnic, it was not that I felt unwelcome on campus - quite the opposite - but I felt the institution was saying to the Chaplaincy, "although we know it is important that you are here, we are not sure why."

Back in 2003, whilst writing a dissertation for an MA in Pastoral Theology, which sought to try and provide something of an answer to that question, I wrote this:

> 'Unlike in a parish, with people who 'belong' to the Church and who give dedicated time to its existence, people in the University belong to a particular office and department which consumes all their interest and time. Chaplaincy is required to tell its story alongside many others, and to do so it is forced to employ the techniques of advertising and marketing beloved of the institution it serves. Immersed in a virtual world, with many students contactable only through cyber-space and required to minister to a mobile, transient community as they pass on street corners and down

corridors, Chaplaincy is well used to trying to find new resources and possibilities to relay its message, and to finding that its 'story' often goes unnoticed.' [2]

So I had to set about the task of trying to equate Gospel and culture; to identify how and why secular, postmodern sound-bites might be given new insight and meaning using the "lens" of Christian faith, theology, and practice; in effect, to invite the university "to try a new language and see if it fits". This process was a reflection of the belief that, far from the proliferation of images and icons that crowd in upon us, which we may feel threaten to declare 'obsolete' the image of the eternal in our lives, those very images are now crying out to their creators to look again at a spirituality which, far from disappearing, speaks anew of God calling us by name.

When Solomon requests from the Lord, 'not riches and honour' but, 'An understanding mind to govern your people, able to discern between good and evil', it is because he feels like a little child, set as he is in the midst of a people that cannot be numbered [I Kings 3v9]. Solomon's wisdom is a recognition that the truth is out there; because the wisdom he is granted is not merely knowledge imposed from above, but an ability to recognise that it is in the culture of the people that surrounds him - amidst the accepted practices and assumptions of the day - that God could still speak to His people and that God's voice might still be heard resonating through all the cultural complexities that was Solomon's inheritance and place in life.

In the series of stories in the Gospels where Jesus tells of what the Kingdom of God is like, they all speak of the 'hiddenness' of the Kingdom. The images He gives us are often interpreted as lessons in humility and patience which need to be learnt. That smallness and insignificance, which are often translated to both our secular and religious lives, will one day have their reward. These little vignettes also provide an image of something Jesus once said when he was in dispute with those who were listening to him. He warned them to realise that the Kingdom of God was not something to which they could point, something imposed magisterially from on high, but it was something already present in the midst of them. It was there in the context of their ordinary, everyday lives waiting to be discovered in and through the gifts, experiences, and tragedies that life often brings. It is hidden amidst a clump of trees providing shelter for the birds of the air; it is leaven, hidden in three measures of flour; it is a priceless pearl found nestling alongside many others. It is in the miracle of the burning bush, on fire with God's presence, yet which is preserved and not consumed.

The choice to study six songs that are embedded in our culture, but may just contain hints and clues which can move us from the transitory to the eternal, is evidence of a process which is not the sole preserve of theology, but also within the world of music: which is a crucial medium enabling us to encounter the transcendent and the numinous. Sometimes it is able to reach and to entrance those who are on the very fringes of faith and has the power to excite, even within the most hard hearted, an awareness of a "spirituality"; a feeling that perhaps, there may be more to this two-dimensional existence that we call life. It may be a sign of the times, that if more and more people are approaching the divine through non-traditional, secular music, then it is no coincidence that the specifically sacred and religious music - especially J. S. Bach - seems to be more available and accessible now than it ever was.

By a cross-pollination of different styles and ages of musical tradition, as well as an endless adaptation of music to other genres - music for films is a good example - the musical world needs no help in demonstrating the power and relevance of the old for the new. Howard Goodall has pointed out that the musical adaptation of the secular for the sacred has old and distinguished roots. Martin Luther's enthusiasm for communal hymn singing led him to collect contemporary folk tunes and adapt them with religious poetry to be sung in Lutheran churches. Many of the songs which have reached the pop chart over the years, and some which have reached the top of it, have either been directly inspired by a religious theme or message, or reflect within their music and lyrics a spiritual dimension which seems more in demand than ever in our twenty-first century. What is attempted here, seeks humbly to emulate that hallowed tradition by taking some contemporary 'folk tunes' and seeing how they might contribute to an understanding of present-day faith and spirituality.

The impetus to write this book also came from a personal perspective. For me music, both popular and classical, both secular and sacred, has been an important instrument of restoration and renewal. All of these songs formed a backdrop for my growing up, and the discovery and exploration of my independence. Not only are they songs which I love to hear, but they all contain music and lyrics which have struck me deeply, emotionally, and intellectually (alongside many others) which may contain a message for our times, and which have been important for me in the progress of my own life.

Even though I was born into a Christian family and have never wandered far from the church, like most other people I have not been spared times when doubt and disbelief have seemed a more attractive alternative; when prayer was indeed languid and faith dim. In 1997, Bishop David Jenkins came to Chelmsford Cathedral to deliver three lectures, called the Keene Lectures, entitled *"Is there a Universal Gospel for the Third Millennium?"* In arguing that Christians are entitled and called to believe in such a thing, he suggested that we have to face the overwhelming case for atheism in order to appreciate its strength and then be more able to confront it. I remember him recounting a story about when he was an undergraduate, hearing the famous expositor of the Gospels R. H. Lightfoot, say in a sermon preached at St. Paul's Cathedral that in the midst of a splendid occasion, surrounded by the great and the good, he was suddenly struck by the apparent futility of it all and said to himself, "'supposing it's all bunk?!'"

Therefore, it is perhaps not surprising that this book reflects on the dialogue between faith and music, which has been so much a part of my faith journey and my professional ministry. It does not matter if the reader is not familiar with any or all of these songs; they have all been vehicles for me to think about the themes presented in this book, but I have used the songs as 'pegs' upon which to hang some thoughts and reflections about issues and challenges that are common to all of us, and which can make our Christian journeys arduous ones. Even with no knowledge of the music and lyrics, merely the title of each song leads the reader into a consideration of the range of human experience that can weigh against the understanding and appreciation of faith and belief in God in today's world, and an exploration of how we might make sense of it.

I feel that all of the songs address, in their own way, what might be termed 'anomie'. A common feeling of powerlessness which, it can be argued, pervades a lot of our modern living. It can be the need to address our loneliness and isolation, or to establish the true colours of who we really are and what we are capable of in the face of an indifferent society prone to misconception and misunderstanding. Amidst the powerlessness engendered by a world so sunk in violence that the threat of annihilation seems an ever present reality, to rediscover positive, life-affirming echoes in the life, teaching, suffering, death, and resurrection of Jesus Christ; to remember again the power of forgiveness, embrace, and redemption which directly confronts that threat of destruction. The fact that six pop songs have been the inspiration for this book is itself a reflection of the task to equate the Gospel with our culture and to rediscover faith in the secular mantle that envelopes us.

There are many reflections and reminiscences in the writing which are echoes of sermons and talks given over the years, and two of the songs, 'Don't Let Me Be Misunderstood' and 'Blowin in the Wind', arose directly out of a requirement to deliver some Good Friday meditations at Chelmsford Cathedral. The meditations delivered to the Nina Simone song were given on Good Friday 2013 and the ones for the Bob Dylan song were rewritten from the ones I originally gave on Good Friday 2002, and which were based on Miroslav Volf's book 'Exclusion and Embrace'.[3] Volf is a Croatian who wrote his book against the backdrop of the Yugoslavian war of 1992 and although magnificent in its scale, it is ultimately an intensely personal book by a man struggling to come to terms with forgiveness, judgement, and love from all that was happening to his native land and his fellow Croats as a result of the savagery unfolding in that land. The book resonated with me deeply and I am indebted to it for influencing much of my thinking for chapter four.

I read it during a project I was undertaking on behalf of the Chaplaincy, to take students and staff from Anglia Ruskin University to Croatia each June and work on the refurbishment of institutions for children and young people with learning difficulties, and to work alongside the Croatian staff working there. Many of the children and young people had been displaced as a result of the fighting, and were as much victims of the war as those who had been killed and injured as a result of the conflict. In fact the songs, 'Blowin in the Wind' and 'Don't Let Me Be Misunderstood', were both written and performed against the backdrop of a turbulent and violent period in the history of the United States, with the Civil Rights Movement and the Vietnam War raging at home and abroad respectively. The songs are a testimony to the power of music, to be able to do what organised religion sometimes cannot or will not do. Sometimes it is the people who we least expect that can prick the conscience of a nation by what they do and by what they sing.

Reflecting on the words of the songs has made me realise, that just as listening to a piece of music or a song can transport one back to a specific memory in a time and a place, so thoughts and concepts, captured and devised at the time, remain deep within the memory and wait to be reawakened, developed, matured, and reapplied to new situations and challenges. In our Christian lives this is important as nothing is lost, nothing is wasted but is given to us, like music itself, as reflective practices and interpretative tools which can be of service to new generations and experiences. So they assist us to journey on that narrow and precipitous path that, we are assured, will one day lead us right into eternal life.

I am grateful to Chelmsford Cathedral and my ministerial colleagues, both for the chance to "test" some of these reflections in the public square and for giving me space and encouragement to write. I owe a huge debt of gratitude to The Revered Canon Andrew Knowles, for his patient reading of the text and for so many helpful corrections and suggestions. Thanks also, to Beverley in the Cathedral Office for her sympathy, patience, and invaluable help wrestling with the computer! Most of all however, thanks to all of those people in my ministry who have, knowingly or not, given me inspiration and insight to enable me to see things clearer than they were before.

Ivor Moody

Don't Let Me Be Misunderstood

Recognising Truth

In 1787 the slavery abolitionist Josiah Wedgewood created what was to become a well known anti-slavery medallion
which depicts a slave; a black figure against a white background
on his knees and bound with a chain, his hands clasped and
raised in a posture of pleading, asking the question 'Am I not a
man and a brother?' Although the image challenges those who
are responsible for the imposition of those chains, its power,
nevertheless, resides in its *passivity*. It is a simple 'handing over'
of humanity to be accepted or rejected by those who share that
humanity. Those who inhabit a common ancestry but who
choose to regard others, because of their nationality, ideology,
or the colour of their skin, as having less of a right to live.

In 1964 Nina Simone sang a song called 'Don't Let Me
Be Misunderstood'. Simone was a child of the Civil Rights
protests and the unrest of fifties and sixties America. She was

herself a victim of the racism and segregation of blacks and whites common to the era. She sang in her church choir and learnt the piano from the age of four, eventually training as a classical pianist. However she failed to win a place at college, claiming later that it was because of the colour of her skin. Ironically, it was this event that turned her to performing folk, blues and jazz music which eventually launched her career and her identification as the voice of the Civil Rights Movement.

Unlike her contemporary Martin Luther King Jr., Simone was an advocate of violent protest to achieve political ends and social change. So it is ironic that the song 'Don't Let Me Be Misunderstood', which many see as a subtext of the Civil Rights Movement, makes an appeal to not misunderstand a soul who is human and who only wishes good for other people. It is an appeal to a different kind of power than that reflected in Josiah Wedgewood's medallion and one which gives us an essential tool for the undertaking of our Christian journeys. The non-violent assertion that despite different appearances, customs and behaviours, and despite the fact that there is good and bad in all of us, we all share a common humanity - an equality of status and a need to be understood that demands tolerance and compassion.

A friend once commented to me that we've all got a PhD in hindsight. It was spoken wistfully, reflecting on so many situations in life when, had it been possible to see the effects of our decisions and behaviours at the time, events might have turned out much more successfully or far less painfully! Just as it is a common human tendency to look to an imagined future that might fulfil all our hopes and desires, so too there is a natural human instinct to reflect on how present knowledge could have shaped and informed past events. The wish to have known then what we know now.

Without the benefit of hindsight however, the Gospels would probably never have seen the light of day. The four accounts we have of Jesus' life, death and resurrection exist only because, for Matthew, Mark, Luke and John, they are not merely attempts to record some of the things Jesus said and did. They are also workings out - catalogues - of how the four evangelists and the early Christian communities whom they were writing for came to realise, with hindsight, what those sayings and actions of Jesus *really* meant. All four accounts are testimonies to how, only when one looks back over the years, does a realisation dawn that our convictions concerning the things of God are, despite all that has happened, clearer than they were.

But of course, this is to imply where now there is more understanding, then there was non-comprehension. The Gospel writers spare no blushes in their descriptions of the misunderstandings of the Roman and Jewish authorities towards Jesus or the disciples who were his friends and companions. The Gospel accounts are packed with false assumptions, misconstrued opinions, and mistaken identities. It is this pattern of misunderstandings about Jesus that often leads to heartache and violence, which hovers like a shadow over his ministry until the cross becomes the ultimate destination for heartache and violence to end up. The Gospels are testimonies of what happens when people so completely misunderstand you that the violence and injustice you suffer is actually based on their false assumptions about who you are and what you are about. What we don't understand we fear; and what we fear we can seek to destroy.

The evidence for the misunderstanding of who and what Christ was, what he was here for, and what he represented is so prevalent in the Gospels, that perhaps its real significance as a contributor to Christ's sufferings has been underplayed. We are familiar with those graphic images of Christ's injuries; suffering and torture that feed our sense of the sheer awfulness of the crucifixion. Before its glorious climax in the Easter Garden, the story of Jesus' Passion delivers the bloody sweat of intense stress and foreboding in the Garden of Gethsemane; the beating; the mockery and the injuries sustained through his trial before Pilate; the falling under the weight of the cross he was forced to carry and to which he was eventually nailed. Then, in a final insult to his broken emaciated body, the stabbing with a spear into his side just to make sure he was dead.

After all of this, the concept of being misunderstood perhaps seems rather an anaemic contributor to those agonies. My contention however is that at least part of what we understand as 'the scandal of the cross' resides not only in the obvious cruel and bloody events which culminated in Christ's death, but that such an earth-shattering, history changing event can trace some of its roots to very ordinary human mistakes and misdemeanours. The implication of misunderstanding another's intentions and purpose, is that within the context of the crucifixion, this rather mild mannered, ineffectual, gently chiding, non-threatening word – misunderstanding - becomes a major player in the drama of the Creator of the world. The hands that flung stars into space and the feet that walked in the first garden at the dawn of time in the cool of the evening, now fastened tightly to the wood of the cross. As such, it can provide an effective 'lens' with which to focus on the opposition and hostility towards Jesus and his suffering on the cross.

Good Intentions...

In a book called 'The Stature of Waiting', William Vanstone has argued that Jesus' arrest in the Garden of Gethsemane is the moment when Jesus' ministry and life turns from activity to passivity - from doing *to and for* others to *being done to by* others. When he talks about the concept of Jesus being 'handed over', he argues that Jesus becomes the object rather than the subject of unfolding events; a waiting figure acted upon, used, who receives passively all that human life can throw at him, divinely dependent and exposed to both the goodness and evil that afflicts him.

Long before Gethsemane however, Jesus had needs and dependencies for which he looked to other human beings around him to provide. The Incarnation was a handing over of the divine into the care of the human; from the moment of Jesus' birth, the Son of God was dependent upon the kindness and tenderness of other human beings. In the midst of so much angelic activity and human travelling to visit and adore the Christ Child, in a phrase of beautiful simplicity, Luke tells us that Mary '*Wrapped* him in bands of cloth, and *laid* him in a manger'. These two gentle, loving actions would have assured the Infant King of both a physical and an emotional stability, not just in the face of the rude, bare surroundings of his birth, but throughout the dangerous refugee status he and his family had to endure in the first days and months of his life. And it was a characteristic that was to accompany him throughout his entire life.

He who created the vault of Heaven tells someone that the Son of Man had nowhere to lay his head. He who assuaged the thirst of an Exodus people, flops down beside a well and asks a Samaritan woman for a drink. He who created a garden in which to walk, enjoys the hospitality of Martha, Mary, Lazarus, and many others who provide for his protection and well-being. Indeed, the task of looking after Jesus and his experience of having those needs fulfilled, may have coloured the way Jesus saw his Heavenly Father answering prayers. 'Is there anyone among you', he asks, 'who if your child asks for bread will give a stone? Or if the child asks for a fish will give a snake?' [Matthew 7:9] Jesus makes it clear that the answers we get to our prayers reveals that God never misunderstands or misinterprets our wants and our needs when we pray, even though we may *frequently* misunderstand or misinterpret the answers we get to our prayers.

Some of Jesus' needs were emotional though and were to do more with his psychology than his body. One of the most revealing and most poignant moments in the Gospels comes in John Chapter 6. The teaching isn't going well, many are taking offence at Jesus' dramatic and uncompromising words and are drifting away including some of the wider circle of his disciples. Then John tells us, 'So Jesus asked the twelve "Do you also wish to go away?"' What a moment that is! It all hangs in the balance and Jesus knows it, the salvation of mankind and the existence of the church dangle by a thread.

The tension here is not just about the precariousness of Jesus' mission and purpose. This heart-stopping question is also a moment of extreme personal anxiety and insecurity. That even his twelve chosen, trusted, beloved companions upon whom he depended and relied; who were his sole friends; who up until now had continued with him in his trials, might *also* want to go away and leave him. It is a moment when Jesus' most intense and complex needs are glimpsed. Here is one of those moments when the shadow of the cross falls over Jesus' ministry and we get a chilling foretaste of that which Christ dreads, becoming terrible in its final manifestation during the story of his Passion.

Franco Zeffirelli's film 'Jesus of Nazareth', which starred Robert Powell, was made in 1980. One section that struck me forcibly when I first saw it was the Last Supper scene. The Gospels tell us that the meal was in an Upper Room and that it had already been made ready for the Passover party to arrive, and John tells us that they were close enough for the Beloved Disciple John to recline on Jesus' breast. What is striking about the film is the effective way it portrays the intimacy which would have been a feature of the occasion. Here is an image of affection and communication between a band of brothers that only years spent with Jesus, experiencing triumph and tragedy, hope and despair and a vision of the highest heaven and the lowest earth could have engendered. It helped me to realise that when Jesus begins the meal by saying, 'I have eagerly desired to eat this Passover with you before I suffer', this was no mere 'school' to teach the disciples what would be the meaning of the new Passover for the embryonic Christian Church. It was an opportunity to be together with people whom Jesus had come to love and who now needed to bear him up and to help him endure the final hours of his life.

Our needs though are not simply the 'stuff' that is necessary to get us through life, whether it is food and drink to keep us alive, work and rest to engage and refresh us, or companionship to help us realise that we are not alone. Our needs also speak about our *identity*; our desire to be needed, to be recognised, and to be valued by those around us. So much of our energy and purposefulness is bound up with the sense of our usefulness to others and the contribution we make to their lives, and to the common ordering of the society in which we find ourselves. In his 'Devotions Upon Emergent Occasions', John Donne's assertion, 'Any man's death diminishes me, because I am involved in mankind' (Meditation 17) doesn't only refer to our common inheritance of flesh and blood, but an insistence that our actions and intentions are precisely for the building up and the edifying of the whole Body of Christ. What we do affects others and their recognition of us, just as what they do affects us and our recognition of them.

One of the chief characteristics of my ministry as vicar of a dockside parish where I served from 1988 to 1996 was the huge number of baptisms, I came to realise that there were two main reasons for this. It was a community which had grown up alongside the docks, although the docks had long since ceased to be the all-encompassing employer it once was, it was a settled, static community which had never seemed to share or enjoy the wealth created by what was once a busy, bustling port. Nevertheless, the town that was adjacent to the docks had deep roots in the area and was fiercely protective of its dockside heritage and the many generations that had become associated with it. Consequently the parish church was synonymous with this historic, settled, static community, and children brought for baptism were seen as contributing to and extending this generational line, this corporate identity, preserving its history and carrying it forward, and I think that was true as much on a community level as it was on an individual one.

The other reason had to do with the economics of the area. Unemployment and degeneration had taken its toll on vision and ambition within the community. There was a real sense of apathy and helplessness in the face of a perceived lack of opportunity, exacerbated by a fair amount of hardship. It came as no surprise then, for this community more than any other I have experienced or in which I have worked, children represented the best and brightest hope for the future. When they were brought for baptism it was not just about the value and sense of worth they brought to all around them, but the sense of continuity and survival they brought with the past and the future. Baptism involves 'naming the names' and in so doing establishing identity, meaning and hope.

Names and identities were central to the call, valuing and commissioning of people in the scriptures whose lives had been intersected by God. Time and again, those who experienced this remember where they were and what they were doing when it happened. It was, 'In the *sixth* month the angel *Gabriel* was sent by God to a town in *Galilee*, called *Nazareth* to a *virgin* engaged to a man whose name was *Joseph*, of the house of *David*. The virgin's name was *Mary*' [Luke 1:26-27]

The narrative makes it clear that part of God's security for his self-emptying resides in the knowledge that many others will know who Jesus is, and his identity is crucial to the unfolding of the story of the Nativity. It brings the shepherds to the manger through the message of the angels. It brings the Wise Men from the East in search of him who is born King of the Jews. The identity of the Christ Child, which they reveal to Herod as the cause of their journey, alerts an earthly king to the potential rivalry of another; and genocide in an attempt to eradicate the threat is the grisly result. The naming and circumcision of Jesus by Simeon at the Temple confirmed his identity to a man who had been waiting all his life for its revealing, but it was to pierce the heart of she whose life had given life to God.

Names not only confirmed people's identity, but they also helped to identify their purpose and the tasks they were called to do. Peter became Cephas; Saul became Paul, and their names linked them to an ancestry that ensured they belonged to something greater than the sum of the parts; to a God who was the God of Abraham, Isaac, and Jacob. Although, of course, Jesus never needed the approval or approbation of human kind, he *did* at least need the disciples, particularly Peter, James, and John, to know who he was and this was a crucial aspect of their training to be Apostles. Accompanying him as closely as they did in his ministry, especially on the Mount of Transfiguration, left them in no doubt as to his identity and his question to Peter 'Who do you say that I am?' is a turning point. The recognition of Jesus' identity becomes the corner stone upon which the Church is to be built, even though the identity of the Messiah is as a suffering servant, a divine being who purposely seeks out the company and love of friends and companions, and who relied on the goodness and generosity of others to grant him shelter and security.

Don't Misunderstand Me...

The opposite of identity is non-being, and that can lead to *annihilation.* The attempt to exterminate the Jews and other communities considered inferior in the Second World War, was an attempt to wipe out a collective identity. Part of the horror of places like Auschwitz, and since 1945 Cambodia, Srebrenica, and elsewhere that display the remains and arte-facts of countless victims who are the result of human killing on an industrial scale, is that they are peoples with no name. Their identities and their right to exist were denied them by those whose own existence was perceived as valid and right-eous. All we know is that they were people, like we are now, and they were people who had an equal right to live.

For Jesus too, the misunderstanding of his identity, first seen in the genocide hours after his birth, loomed through-out his ministry and always threatened to raise the spectre of non-being and annihilation. What makes the concept of misunderstanding Jesus' needs and identity fundamental to an understanding of the true meaning and horror of Golgotha, is that it is not merely evidenced in the arguments and con-frontations he had with his opponents. It also came from the inside out - from those closest to him - trusted loved ones and companions that reflects the agony of the psalmist:

"It is not enemies who taunt me - I could bear that;
  it is not adversaries who deal insolently with me - I

could hide from them. But it is you, my equal, my companion, my familiar friend, with whom I kept pleasant company; we walked in the house of God with the throng." [Psalm 55:12-14]

The only story we have of Jesus' childhood is in Luke's Gospel from when he was twelve. He stayed behind in Jerusalem questioning the Scribes, Pharisees, and doctors of the law whilst his parents set off on the long journey home. The story centres on his parents' misunderstanding of their son's identity. When they eventually find him in the Temple and chide him he says to them, 'Did you not know that I must be in my Father's house?' Luke adds, tellingly, 'But they did not understand what he said to them' [Luke 2:41-50]. Jesus' retort to them is that if they had fully understood, it would have explained why he was where he was.

That misunderstanding was to assume ominous proportions later in a story from St. Mark's Gospel. At the height of Jesus' teaching and healing ministry, when many unclean spirits were being cast out, Mark includes a little uncomfortable detail about Jesus, his family, and his circumstances that Matthew and Luke omit - as they sometimes do when they re-tell stories that Mark recounted first. He mentions that in the middle of it all, Jesus returns home and his family come to restrain him, 'For people were saying "He has gone out of his mind"'. [Mark 3:19b-21] When Mary, Joseph, and his family come to collect Jesus and take him away, it isn't just that they expect to care for a son, that they would now barely recognise, who had changed forever; this is a King now turned madman. It is the *worst kind* of non-being. What promised to be the ultimate in greatness seems to be the opposite. He has become a parody, a sham, of the identity he claimed for himself.

The assumption about Jesus' mental health from within

the bosom of his family radiates out into the community of which he and his family is a part, and here it takes on a confrontational aspect. He comes to the Synagogue at Nazareth to begin his ministry by declaring himself as the fulfilment of Isaiah's prophecy; that captives would be released, the blind would recover their sight, and the poor would have the Good News preached to them. The reaction of the townsfolk reveals their catastrophic misunderstanding of who Jesus is and what he is about:

> "Where did this man get all this? Is not this the carpenter, the son of Mary and brother of James and Joses and Judas and Simon, and are not his sisters with us? And they took offense at him."
> [Mark 6:1-3]

Faced with Jesus' claim that he is the fulfilment of Isaiah's prophecy, the indignant question of those in the synagogue that day, 'Who does this man think he is?' becomes 'This man *thinks* he is - but we know different - we know better.' In Luke's version of this story, in their rage at the claims he makes for himself, they take him to the edge of the cliff to throw him off and Jesus directly faces that annihilation which is the result of having one's identity challenged and misunderstood; an event that was another foreshadowing of Good Friday.

We have observed two primary misunderstandings of Jesus which weave their way throughout the Gospels and which centre upon his identity; a failure to comprehend his human needs and desires as the Incarnate Son of God, and the true nature of his mission as God's Son. It is in the final hours of Jesus' life where these misunderstandings come to play a defining role in his destiny, and they are perpetrated by those who were closest to Jesus' heart.

Earlier, the Last Supper was portrayed as an occasion of intimacy between Jesus and his disciples; a chance for the Master to gather with his closest friends so that they could draw mutual strength and support in preparation for impending events. However, the Last Supper was also a crisis of misunderstanding and misconception about who and what Jesus was. In the midst of all Jesus' teaching over the bread and wine about love, about death, about resurrection, and about heaven, there is also tension, exasperation, and despair that his disciples would *never* understand, or *never* realise the truth. In Luke's Gospel, Jesus summons his disciples in the face of extreme provocation and trial to take their faith and their courage and to love to the limit: 'But now, the one who has a purse must take it, and likewise a bag. And the one who has no sword must sell his cloak and buy one'. The challenge is met though, with only tragic, complete misunderstanding. The disciples take him literally and interpret Jesus' words not as an exhortation to go the extra mile for peace, but as a call to arms. Excitedly they cry 'Lord, look! Here are two swords!' Jesus' despairing response is a lashing out in frustration that we can all recognise, "It is enough!" [Luke 22:35-38]. Nina Simone's secular appeal in her song, "Don't Let Me Be Misunderstood", is a plea which crosses the centuries and offers us an expression which helps us to draw close to the despairing, suffering heart of God.

The account of the Last Supper in John's Gospel is a narrative that is peppered with anxious, persistent questions layered one on top of another [John 13:36-16:30]. First it was Peter who asked, 'Lord where are you going?' closely followed by Thomas who says, 'Lord we do not know where you are going. How can we know the way?' Then comes Philip's misguided request, 'Lord show us the Father and we will be satisfied' and the sense of Jesus' exasperation and despair is palpable. 'Have I been with you all this time Philip, and you *still* do not know me?' Then comes Judas' question, 'How is it that you will reveal yourself to us and not to the world?' Finally, it is all the disciples who puzzle over Jesus' ultimate destination; 'What does he mean by saying to us, "A little while and you will no longer see me, and again a little while and you will see me"?…We do not know what he is talking about'.

This Upper Room dialogue has a dramatic quality in its relentless questioning and answering, and it is possible to perceive a build - up in tension, excitement, and expectancy, until there is an explosion of apparent certainty - that *now* Jesus has made everything clear, that *finally* they understand, that *finally* the truth has manifested itself. 'Yes, *now* you are speaking plainly', his disciples say, 'Not in any figure of speech! Now we know that you know all things, and do not need to have anyone question you; by this we believe that you came from God'. This exclamation reads like a sigh of relief in the text, a deep exhaling of re-assurance and satisfaction that here, at last, is the answer to all those competing claims to truth; all those jostling and clashing narratives that seem to befuddle and confuse. The disciples' quest for certainty, to have everything clear, to have achieved a comfortable truth and to have reached a status quo seemed to have been realised.

The acquisition of certainty though can be a substitute for when the pain and challenge of the *real* truth is too difficult or uncomfortable to comprehend, and Jesus reveals it. 'Do you now believe?' asks Jesus, 'The hour is coming, indeed it has come, when you will be scattered, each one to his home, and you will leave me alone'. And it is in the Garden of Gethsemane where all this takes on a final reality. For he who knew the security, and safety of swaddling cloths and a mother's loving arms at his greatest hour of need the true plaintiveness of Christ's question to Peter and the sleeping disciples is witnessed, 'Are you *still* sleeping and taking your rest? Could you not stay awake with me one hour?'

It is impossible to know for certain what the trigger was for

Judas' betrayal of Jesus, perhaps it was for monetary gain. In St. John's Gospel, Judas is identified as a thief who used to steal from the common purse, and the promise of thirty pieces of silver for his betrayal of Jesus to the chief priests - a lot of money - would have been a tempting prospect indeed. Judas' betrayal might *also* have been an attempt to force Jesus' hand; to bring him 'out in the open' and compel him to declare a charismatic leadership that would oust the Roman occupiers and re-establish the sovereignty of Israel. Whatever his motives however, the pathos of the question to Judas in the garden, 'Judas, is it with a kiss that you are betraying the Son of Man?' cries out for us to recognise that this is both the betrayal of Christ's mission and purpose, and the betrayal of a friend; someone who, privileged though he was to have had Jesus' love and affection lavished upon him, chooses a level of intimacy borne of that companionship to effect his betrayal.

And now with the dawning of the awful truth, the disciples all forsake Jesus. Peter is left to weep bitterly; Judas is left hanging from a tree; for the rest of the characters involved in the story of Christ's Passion and death, their behaviour becomes a testimony to what is the ultimate destination of misunderstanding and non-comprehension. Part of the awful inevitability of the cross is that Jesus' silence and stillness in front of his accusers and his going like a lamb to the slaughter, is borne of a wisdom that recognises when there is misunderstanding to the point where a situation appears to be unchangeable or irredeemable, then there is a sense of powerlessness, because any attempt to try and put things right seems futile.

Reaching Understanding...

So where does all this leave us? So far we have a catalogue of evidence to suggest that the concept of being misunderstood which is so much a feature of our humanity, is a major factor in the task to try and understand a little more about the life and death of Jesus Christ. But to understand the significance of being misunderstood doesn't just take us up to the cross, it also helps us to see *beyond* it. The misunderstanding of the truth of Jesus Christ may have played a crucial part in driving him to his cross, but in the end all it did, was to allow love's redeeming work to be done.

For Mary Magdalene, in the garden, the risen Christ was mistaken for a gardener and yet the empty tomb reveals the ultimate truth of Christ as Lord of life and death. The misunderstanding of Christ's needs, so prevalent before Good Friday, are now redeemed and restored through the greeting and the clasping of his feet by one who loved him, and who could once again show him the love and affection for which he had craved. The miraculous draught of fish as a result of the stranger on the shore telling them to try once more letting down their nets for a catch, reveals the ultimate truth of Christ as Lord of creation. As Peter leaps into the water at the Beloved Disciple's recognition of who this stranger was, so the misunderstanding of Christ's identity is redeemed and restored.

The story of the Emmaus Road is one of bereavement. It is a lament for the loss of someone very precious by two of his closest friends, but it is also a testimony to where the misunderstanding of someone's purpose and message can lead: to a loss of vision and a sense of despair, that because of apparently getting it all wrong and misconstruing what they thought the future might hold, that all that promise and hope had come to nothing. The expression of grief is for,

'Jesus of Nazareth, who was a prophet mighty in deed
and word before God and all the people, and how
our chief priests and leaders handed him over to be

condemned to death and crucified him. But we had hoped that he was the one to redeem Israel.' [Luke 24:13-35]

When the stranger who had joined them on the Emmaus Road accepted their invitation to join them for an evening meal, he performs the great Eucharistic act that was forever to define the church; by taking the bread, blessing it, breaking it and then distributing it to the two disciples. By doing so he reveals his identity as the wounded healer, Jesus Christ the Lord of the Church, and so for the two disciples the misunderstanding of Christ's purpose is redeemed and restored. They testify, both to themselves and to the infant church back in Jerusalem, to which they return with joy, 'Were not our hearts burning within us, while he was talking to us on the road, while he was opening the scriptures to us?'

Here is revealed the true power of the cross. A tendency to misunderstand, which might formerly have contributed to our condemnation, works instead through the cross for our salvation and assures us that the final destination for all our Christian journeys will be a glorious one. No matter how impatient and intolerant we become to others and to God because of our inability to make sense of our faith and the meaning and place of the divine in our lives, nothing lies outside the ability of God to redeem and transform. This is our ultimate assurance that even though human beings will continue to misunderstand truth and reap the chaos and wreckage that frequently results from it, that because of the Good Friday event the final consequence of all our attempts to understand will not be pain, but joy.

True Colours

Finding Strength

'True Colours' was a song written by Billy Steinberg and Tom Kelly in 1986. The song originally concerned Steinberg's mother, for whom one verse and the chorus was written, appealing to her not to be the person so many others wanted her to be, but instead to be the beautiful, authentic person Steinberg knew she could be. Kelly encouraged Steinberg to re-write the song to give it a more universal appeal, taking it away from its very personal origins. It became a lyric in the shape of a simple Gospel style ballad that spoke of *everyone's* need to be themselves, and to come out from behind masks of pretension and to discover their 'true colours'.

'True Colours' has been recorded by several artists (most notably Cyndi Lauper who sang it originally and whose powerful and original performance made it a worldwide hit). One of the most poignant and evocative versions was by Eva Cassidy in an album of songs called 'Simply Eva' which was first published in January 2011, fifteen years after her premature death from cancer at the age of thirty three. Up to her death in 1996 she was virtually unknown outside of her native Washington D.C.; it was only years later that she was 'discovered' and her beautiful voice became a global sensation.

Its exhortation to the listener is to not be afraid to be themselves and despite heartache, darkness, and self-doubt to show the world who they really are and what they can really do. The song also has much to say to those whose faith, in themselves and in God, seems so languid in the face of lives which appear fruitless and without meaning. It could have been a biography of Eva herself; someone whose true colours, apparently hidden and robbed by the cruel disease which ended her life, finally break through and reveal to the world the enormous talent which was hers. Here is a contemporary language of death and resurrection which resonates powerfully with the message of the Gospel, and which is a powerful partner supporting us as we undertake our Christian journeys.

We began by looking at the most significant Christian journey of all, Jesus Christ's own to the cross and beyond. If we are to try and make sense of some of the trials and tribulations that beset us on our Christian journeys, we can do no better than see them set within the context of the trials and tribulations of He who embarked on the first Christian journey. The Master who inspires us and calls us to undertake our own adventure.

We saw in the last chapter that it is possible to decipher not one, but a catalogue of misunderstandings throughout Jesus' sojourn on earth; about who he was and what he was here for. A 'steady flow' of questionings, disputes, and challenges about his status, purpose, and mission that really turns the spotlight to where a steady chipping away of confidence and certainty can lead. A process that reaches its peak in the Garden of Gethsemane with Jesus' agonised request to his Heavenly Father that the cup of suffering pass him by.

If what has been stated is right about the misunderstanding of Jesus being underrated in its culpability for Jesus' suffering, then this cry of desperation is not just one wrought by the fear of impending pain. It is a human reaction with which we can all equate, but it is also an expression of a crushing self-doubt. A monumental crisis of identity that, in the end, after all had been said and done, he had been in the wrong all along and his opponents right, and so he just ought to forget it and go home.

Insignificance...

When people encourage us to show our 'true colours', what they usually mean, is that often in the face of some difficulty or obstacle, we need to show what we are made of and what we have the potential to achieve. To be able to demonstrate a self-confidence and an ability that will overcome.

The singer of the song 'True Colours' is serenading a friend for whom life has just become too much. She knows her friend has hidden depths, buried under the rubble of many toils and cares, and seeks to give her reassurance; although others may not realise it or believe it to be true, she sees her friend's 'true colours' clearly visible through all the dust and smoke.

Over the years though, I have met many people whose response to the Gospel and the call to live the Christian life has been hamstrung by an immense sense of inadequacy or unworthiness. They have found it difficult to foster any self-belief that as Christians they can cause God to act with their prayers and through their suffering, buried as it is under the weight of worldly toils, cares, and often the fear of what others might think if their faith were to become public knowledge. 'Say one for me vicar' is a request for prayer often made by those 'outside' the church or on the fringes of faith which will be familiar to Christians and ministers wherever they serve and witness. The call to be of service to others in this way is implicitly recognised in such requests, and it should be met with joyful compliance and a rejoicing that here is someone groping their way to a closer walk with God. However, I have always felt a tinge of sadness when presented with them, because what is *also* implicit is the assumption that somehow one's own prayer is not good enough. More powerful 'magic' is needed from those in the know and those who have been pronounced worthy by the church. One of the greatest impediments to our Christian journey, let alone to the undertaking of any mission and evangelism, is the crushing of the human spirit; and that is something that takes us close to the heart of Christ in Gethsemane.

Yet it is both to society and to the church where we must look for a rationale for that state of mind. Despite all of our modern day awareness of equality and diversity issues, and our secular sound bites trumpeting independence, self-sufficiency, and equal rights, the fact remains, that centuries of theology and spirituality emphasizing our inadequacy in the face of an omnipotent creator who is justly angered by our sins, has taken its toll. It is alive and well in many of the liturgies we say and sing in our churches today. In the hymn 'There is a Green Hill Far Away', one verse states:

> *There was no other good enough*
>
> *To pay the price of sin;*
>
> *He only could unlock the gate*
>
> *Of heaven, and let us in.*

To those countless people today who are convinced that the illness or calamity that has befallen them has something to do with a God who is punishing them for their iniquity, there has been a drip-feed of a divine blame culture. This was given wings by St. Anselm in the Middle Ages by portraying an outraged God whose magisterial existence has been challenged and abused by the sin of the women and men he had created. An outrage only assuaged by the death of Christ, a ransom paid by Jesus with his blood, as a satisfaction for sin not to Satan who held the world in chains, but to his angry and offended heavenly father.

The trouble with all of this is that it overlooks the fact that salvation was not just procured *for* us, it was achieved *with* us. The choice of a young girl to bear the Christ Child and the calling of her unborn son 'Emmanuel', which means 'God with us', meant that the whole purpose of the Incarnation was to *involve* mankind in the process of its own salvation.

Jesus courts rejection and ridicule when he dines with tax collectors and sinners, and when he welcomes the outcast into his company, precisely so that he can inhabit their brokenness. Jesus once told the Scribes and the Pharisees who were outraged that he chose to eat with tax collectors and sinners, that it was the sick who needed a doctor, not those who were well. Jesus makes it clear in his ministry that his disciples are the ones who have been called from their fishing nets to fish for people. They are the ones who have continued with him in his trials, their status was not as servants but trusted friends. They are not mere passive observers in the battle between good and evil which was being played out in an occupied, impoverished and dispossessed little nation in first century Palestine.

The perception of our 'true colours', as those abilities and qualities we have in order to overcome what may seem to be insurmountable problems and barriers is hampered though, not only by our view of God's relationship with us but by our relationships with each other. When Jesus was confronted by sickness or sin there would have been an acute awareness, not only of present symptoms but also past traumas. A holistic care and concern for the person that would have taken into account what it was that had placed them now in Jesus' presence. We know all too well that society does not always rest comfortably with disease and disability, and many people go to great lengths to hide their physical or mental pain, not only because of a natural fear about what the end result of their suffering might be, but because of the stigma that may be attached to their infirmity. If we are reticent about discussing or confessing our maladies, it is a reticence exacerbated by society's general inability to readily accept 'difference'.

In 1973, BBC Radio 4 broadcast a programme called 'Does he take sugar?' which focussed on disability issues and public attitudes towards them. The programme sparked a global interest in the subject, with other countries doing similar media awareness raising campaigns to highlight the issues. The phrase, 'Does He Take Sugar?' has become a strapline for campaigners seeking to spotlight poor practice resulting from prejudice against 'difference', whether it be gender, race or disability.

One of my first encounters with a student, soon after I had started as the Chaplain on Anglia Ruskin University's Chelmsford Campus, was with a woman in her late 30's. Trained ostensibly for parish ministry, after fifteen years in the job, I found myself in an environment which was very far from my comfort zone. It was with a sense of desperation at not knowing where to start with my ministry as a Chaplain in this Higher Education institution, that one day I plonked myself down next to this woman in the student bar to try and find out what made people 'tick' in this vibrant, stressful community. Tentatively I asked her why, at this stage in her life, she had come to study at University. She looked at me for a long time and then said to me, 'I have been married for ten years, I have two small children and my husband has told me consistently that I have no brain and that my place is at the kitchen sink. I have come here to prove that bastard wrong!'

Writing about so many students at Anglia Ruskin University who had to overcome enormous obstacles like stigma, prejudice, disability or low self-esteem to get to University and gain their qualification, my former Chaplaincy colleague Malcolm Guite wrote:

'The world notices and praises the rich, the powerful, the talented, those who are seen to be at what the world thinks is the centre of things. The world chooses to ignore or overlook the weak, the self-doubting and those on what the world deems to be on the margins of life. For the Kingdom it is just the other way round. The most exciting things happen on the margins, when the eyes of the powerful are turned the other way. The grace and love of God flow most clearly into the world in and through the lives of the weak.' [4]

So much of Jesus' ministry takes place on the borders of communities and districts because that is where the ostracised people are; people despised and excluded because of race, culture, creed, and specifically because of their disease. It is on the border between Samaria and Galilee, in a lonely place far from civilisation, where Jesus passes by a colony of lepers and the fact that they call out to him to attract his attention testifies to their 'untouchable' status. They realise who this person is, but *still* they do not approach him, preferring to shout across the distance, not just because of the fear of the contagion of others but because of the social stigma under which they were placed [Luke 17: 11-19].

The seat of power in this story lies not in the cleansing of their leprosy or in the showing of themselves to the priests so that they would be re-integrated back into society. It is found when the one thankful leper crosses the distance that separated them to return to Jesus and fall at his feet. It is more than just gratitude, it is an outpouring of all the agony of the disease, the shame of being unclean, and the stigma of being ostracised, which would have put an intolerable mental and physical burden on this little lamb of God. It is a cleansing in the broadest sense of the term, because its a revealing of a tortured soul for whom so much would have remained unsaid, *until now*.

Not for nothing did Jesus require the woman healed of her twelve year haemorrhaging which would have classed her as unclean, to come and declare *why* she had touched the fringe of his garment. Of course it was a lesson in the power of faith to all the bystanders and those pressing in upon Jesus; but it was also a recognition that so much more had been exposed and healed than merely the physical malady that had incapacitated and impoverished her [Mark 5: 24b-34]. It was only the presence of the Good Shepherd who could truly understand and excise all the hidden, unspeakable, and unnameable pain hidden deep down inside one of his treasured flock. In the Gospels, at the feet of Jesus is the place where there is frequently a final, and humble recognition that the reasons for finding oneself kneeling there were often iceberg like in size and complexity. That what is presented to us in the Gospels is merely the tiny visible part of a vast, submerged, and complicated story.

There are things about our lives that we think lie dormant within us, or which we go to great lengths to suppress, but actually drive us and determine our behaviour for large portions of our time. The woman who crashes the Pharisees' meal where Jesus is a guest, silently performs her penitential act of love by washing Jesus' feet with her tears and drying them with her hair. This devotional display was more than just deep sorrow for her sins. It was a reflection of the fact that her pain and anguish at a life spent trying to stave off poverty and trying to endure stigma and scorn was such that words were too inadequate to express the depth of her sadness. Her story is truly one that demonstrates that actions can indeed speak louder than words [Luke 7: 36-50].

Blindness...

Yet what was true of an individual's confinement - inhibiting them from the best that they could be and the fullest person that they were - was also true, on a collective level, of the Jewish nation itself. Jesus Christ was condemned to death not only because he was an upstart who had threatened to destroy the Temple and rebuild it in three days, or because he was considered a blasphemer who had claimed to be God's Son. Jesus had uncovered a national *sickness,* a combined repressed pain borne of foreign occupation and exile stretching from his present time back hundreds of years, which had damaged national identity and pride. These were historical events which had shaped and defined the Jewish people, revealing that their behaviour and outlook was profoundly affected by past events and traumas. The need to protect and preserve religious and doctrinal purity in the face of relentless conquest and occupation would have been instrumental in the making and despising of outcasts - the very people whom Jesus befriended and exalted - to preserve and protect national identity and purpose. It was the driving force behind a national, often violent behaviour, to make restitution for past ills and slights and to preserve pride and heritage in the face of the threat of annihilation; and it proved to be a blinding, obsessive instigator of human behaviour.[5]

It would have been easy to vent cathartic anger at some-one who told stories like the Good Samaritan, who had the temerity to suggest that the Sabbath was the best day of all to release someone from their bondage to pain, and who dared to deliver the message that it was better to love your enemies and to return hatred with kindness. Jesus' relentless progress to Golgotha is the final manifestation of people's anger and pain, which come together to give true meaning and force to the Old Testament reference to a 'scapegoat' - a bearer of all the sins, inadequacies and pains of so many others [Leviticus 16: 20-21, Isaiah 53:6]. At the cross, the taunts and accusations aimed against Jesus are the expression of a corporate pain, which expresses itself through the blind anger and hatred of those who became the nation's mouthpiece.

And all of this made *Jesus* angry, because in exposing the 'true colours' that drove a nation's outlook and behaviour, the nature of the repression of an individual's true colours became easier to see. It was an intense indignation that helped to drive Jesus to the cross because he knew that things could not stay as they were, and that something final, transformative, and life changing needed to be achieved. The drawing out of people's long held and deeply felt pain was the action of a shepherd whose compassion was fuelled by the same righteous anger as that of the Good Samaritan - who was drawn across the road by the callous savagery with which he was faced. Some com-mentators suggest that there is an identification to be made between Jesus and the hero of his own story. Compassion is not merely defined as feeling sorry for someone, it is emblem-atic of a righteous anger that such a cruel injustice has been done to one of God's children. There was in Jesus an intense anger that evil in one form or another seemed responsible for the pain, stigma, and rejection which had indelibly tinged the lives of so many people for so long. It is a passion borne of compassion, teased out by the parlous state of mankind; harassed and dejected little lambs like sheep without a shepherd, buffeted by capricious events and assaulted by direct attacks upon goodness.

When a man with a withered hand presents himself in the Synagogue on the Sabbath in St. Mark's Gospel, Jesus' exasperation with the situation is plain to see. 'Is it lawful to do good or to do harm on the Sabbath, to save life or to kill?' he asks those who were watching with malevolent intent, 'To see whether he would cure him on the Sabbath, so that they might accuse him'. The Evangelist, St. Mark, gives us a precious detail that the other Evangelists omit in their reporting of the same story. He tells us that Jesus, 'Looked round at them with anger; he was grieved at their hardness of heart' [Mark 3vv1-6].

Luke tells us, when Jesus was confronted in the Synagogue by a woman who, 'Was bent over and was quite unable to stand up straight', his anger was directed to Satan who had kept this 'Daughter of Abraham' bound 'for eighteen long years'. This crucial detail testifies to the longevity of the suffering that this woman had endured, which all at once would have been physical, mental, and societal. Jesus was also angry that the literal interpretation of the Jewish law by the religious authorities was also contributing to the longevity of the suffering witnessed by him on this day, which also made them the subject of his attention. 'You hypocrites!' cries Jesus, outraged that people will untie their ox or donkey and lead them from the manger to give them water on the Sabbath day, but object when a human being has the prospect of being untied from her bondage on a day that is made for human kind and not the other way round! [Luke 13vv10-17]

And with righteous anger comes deserved judgement. If the uncovering of our 'true colours' is about all we can be and do, then the capacity for evil is exposed along with the ability for good; the wheat and the tares discovered nestling and growing together. Occasionally I have been asked what I would do if I met Jesus today, and I know the answer to that; I would run away and hide. It is not that I wouldn't be intensely curious, like Zacchaeus who climbed a tree so that he could see Jesus; or hungry for a sign like the five thousand who ate their fill of the loaves. But I would be scared, because if Jesus caught my gaze there would be nothing about me hidden from him and my true colours would be laid bare. His intense understanding of me would entail judgement, and a response from me that I fear - like the rich young man who was challenged by Jesus to sell all he had and give it to the poor as a precursor to following Jesus - would send me away shocked and grieving because, like him, I have many possessions. When we read or listen to the story of Christ's Passion, we participate but with a kind of painful, uneasy detachment. Not because we are removed from the action, but because the *opposite* is true. We shade our eyes, hardly daring to come out from behind the sofa because we know that in the face of such awfulness and pain, such apparent, abject failure, we would have fled long before nails were driven into hands and feet.

One of the stark brutalities of the cross is that its remorseless exposure of the Son of God to suffering and death draws people to a spectacle from which there is no escape; it offers no hiding place. It is easy to 'sanitize' the cross and sidestep its power to scandalize and offend. We dilute a primary message of the Gospels if we fail to realise that a fundamental characteristic implicit in the mission and message of he who hung upon the cross is a judgement upon all those with whom he came into contact. By virtue of who and what he was, he exposed *their* true colours and showed them that there was nothing hidden that would not be brought into the light.

At the Last Supper, Jesus gazed deeply into Judas' eyes and says, 'Do quickly what you are going to do'. It is easy to assume that Jesus' words to Judas are simply a mandate for him to leave and pursue the progress of his betrayal. However, I wonder whether in that deep, all-consuming eye contact between the Master and his disciple if there was such a complete knowledge and judgement of Judas and what he was about to do, that Judas had no choice but to leave the upper room and all his friends, and that his continuing proximity to all that he had held dear up to that point was no longer bearable or sustainable.

There is the same exposure to judgement, and the same summing up of the 'true colours' that makes the man, as there is when after the cock crowed and Peter's three fold betrayal was complete, 'The Lord turned and looked at Peter. Then Peter remembered…' We know what a terrifying, all-knowing, all-consuming gaze that must have been, judging by Peter's reaction. He left the scene and cried the tears of a broken heart. [Luke 22: 54-62]

Encouragement…

Here though, we arrive at that bittersweet irony that defines and affirms our belief in God's purpose and love for us; the fulcrum point for our faith. In the last chapter we saw that the process of misunderstanding, which can throw much light onto the causes of Christ's journey to the cross, becomes not an end in itself, but a transition point which carries us beyond the cross to a new understanding of Christ's identity and purpose. Now, in the very revealing of our true colours there is a pointer to our salvation and the promise of a glorious end to our journey. Seeing someone's true colours is not only about the people they are now, but a realisation of what they *could* become one day. When Jesus assures his disciples that every hair on their heads is counted, it wasn't just an assurance of God's total *knowledge* of them but an assurance of his total *care* for them. The power of the cross resides in its ability to draw out from people the best that they can be, brought about by taking them to the edge, so that they have nowhere else left to run.

Significantly, it can be seen amidst those very outcasts and observers who surround the cross and who are primarily responsible for Jesus' suffering and death. Peter's grief and guilt after the full impact of his three-fold denial of his friendship with Jesus becomes clear and he appears to be inconsolable. But his repentance is borne of a broken heart rendered thus because in the turning and looking of the Lord upon Peter and Peter remembering his promise, there is a deep and lasting realisation that he is loved beyond measure. Every hair on his head has been counted, and that before he was ever formed in the womb, Jesus knew him. Even before Peter's betrayal takes place, Jesus assures him that precisely the same task given to him all those years ago, when by the lakeside Jesus called him and said to him 'Follow me, and I will make you fish for people', will still apply *after* Peter's three fold denial of Jesus. There lies the source of all our repenting, forgiving, and loving.

It is the confession of his crimes that turns one of the malefactors crucified with Jesus into the repentant thief. The remorseless exposure of the cross, in the same moment as it convicts him of the justice of his fate, convinces him too of the injustice of the fate of Jesus. In a moment where the true colours of a human being are forced irresistibly into the light, the thief says, 'Lord, remember me when you come into your kingdom'. It is a similar crunch time moment that confronts the Centurion, witnessing all of these things first hand. He had played Pilate's game and stuck a crown of thorns and a purple robe onto what they thought was a fake king. He had denied even Jesus' most basic need for dignity by stripping him naked and auctioning off his seamless robe. He had played along with the Jews by helping to construct a parody of what the expected Davidic Messiah would be like. But now at the foot of the cross, at the moment of Jesus' death when the suffering and the pain seems to be at its most acute and its most poignant, there comes a moment of insight and revelation - a flash of true colours - and the Centurion realises and declares Jesus' true identity.[6]

The effect is often spectacular and glorious, because if our true colours define who we are in God's sight; beautifully, wonderfully, uniquely created, upon whose heads every hair has been counted, then bearing the cross in our lives also brings out a creative potential. These are our true colours, comprised of extraordinary, courageous, sacrificial behaviour that reveals humanity at its strident best. The Gospels are peppered with people who, when they come into contact with Jesus, discover hidden depths and new strengths about themselves. This sometimes made Jesus *gasp* at the extent of the insight and durability they displayed. The story of the lawyer who tells Jesus that obedience to the two primary commandments - to love God and to love your neighbour as yourself - is more important than any number of offerings and sacrifices, elicits a response from Jesus that pays fitting tribute to the suddenly manifested true colours of the man. 'You', says Jesus, 'Are not far from the Kingdom of God' [Mark 12: 28-34]. It is such a transformative moment that everybody else realises that something revelatory and life changing has happened, and the exchange is greeted by the awed bystanders not with questions, but only silence.

The story of a Roman Centurion who tells Jesus that he need not come to his house to heal his servant, but can instead do it from where he stands makes Jesus turn around to the crowds and exclaim: 'I tell you, not even in Israel have I found such faith!', Jesus' amazement and delight is centred on the fact that a potential tragedy has been averted by a faith which has been matured by the fires of anxiety and suffering. This is a story told by Matthew and Luke, and subtle differences in each account give us rich layers of detail and interpretation. Matthew tells us that the servant is lying paralysed and in 'terrible distress'. Luke tells us that this servant is 'valued highly' by the Centurion, a relationship defined by more than simply monetary or practical considerations. The implication is that there is a genuine closeness and affection between master and servant; so much so, that many observers that day and principally Jesus himself, could see the true colours of this righteous foreigner. For this Centurion too, it seems, there had been a moment of revelation, when his back was against the wall, that truly, this man was the Son of God [Luke 7: 1-10, Matthew 8: 5-13].

In the last chapter it was suggested that the very human activity of his friends looking after Jesus and providing for his needs may have coloured the way he then taught others about how and why God answers our prayers. So perhaps in this chapter we can say that our ability for faith and compassion helped to shape his, our passions gave his added meaning and significance. Our sheer capacity to be strong, to endure, and to love, often in the face of seemingly impossible odds, would have helped Jesus to endure and to have gone to his death knowing all that loving was worth the cost. In short, our 'true colours' would have helped to convince Jesus that by inhabiting our lives, by seeing what we are capable of, and the impetus and stimuli we have that govern why we are capable of them, Jesus is empowered to show his *own* magnificent 'true colours' through his death on the cross.

As we undertake our Christian journeys, to talk of humanity's 'true colours' is to accept that travelling can be burdensome, we toil under a weight of past hurts and pains, and unfulfilled desires and dreams. It is also to realise what we are capable of as human beings, and that the longed for destination in the far distance is achievable despite everything that would hinder our progress. When we read all the Gospel stories of people whose lives were changed and transformed for good, it becomes easier to understand why they were written down, read, and passed around those early Christian communities, and why they continue to be efficacious for us now.

When Jesus brings to light for the Woman of Samaria, by the well at Sychar, that her messy, complicated life is instrumental not in her condemnation but in her acceptance as a little lamb of God, that messy complicated life is also all of ours. When a woman, bent double, is called to the front of the Synagogue to have eighteen years of suffering brought to an end, the longevity of that pain and its responsibility for so much hidden, silent suffering, is all of ours. When at the cross, those individuals through their mocking taunts not only express the fear of a nation, but the discomfort of having been exposed to Jesus' gaze and the deepest secrets of their hearts revealed; the forgiveness requested for them by the Son, to the Father, is for all of us.

One of the characteristics of our humanity is an incredible ability to hang on to the merest sliver of hope in the midst of all else that seems to spell nothing but darkness and suffering. When as the song implies, we can be driven to the edge of craziness and despair by the world in which we inhabit and we feel we can't take any more. It establishes a true redemptive hope that a world seemingly sunk in hopeless betrayal, violence, and darkness is never far from the Kingdom of God. What it means is that the exposure of our beautiful, rainbow-like 'true colours' is not ultimately for our condemnation, but for our salvation.

IVOR MOODY
Songs for
the Soul
•
3

Message in a Bottle

Making Intercession

In 1979, a band called The Police had their only number one chart hit in the UK. It was a song called 'Message in a Bottle', and for the band members themselves the song was a favourite amongst all they had produced. The song tells the tale of a man - described as a castaway marooned on an island - whose loneliness is so painful that he resorts to the desperate attempt of communicating by a message in a bottle, to somebody, anybody, who might respond compassionately to his plight. It speaks of loneliness with melancholic accuracy. One day he comes to the shoreline and sees billions of bottles, just like his, washed up on the beach.

A message in a bottle is both an act of desperation and a gesture of hope. It expresses a human desire to be in touch when there is neither the means nor the time for any other method of communication. It is also an act of faith, produced in the belief that someone, somewhere, someday, *might* find our message in a bottle. The song refers to billions of bottles, each containing a personalised story of loss or despair, but the song envisages a common shore upon which they all get washed up. Against all the odds they come together, united by a common grief and the hope that someone gets the messages they hold inside. Christianity is familiar with that concept.

I have never thought of heaven as a kind of fairytale utopia, but it might not be unreasonable to imagine it as a shore that is big enough and safe enough to absorb people's pain. A place where hope and joy is communicated through the promise that we are not alone. So a song, which speaks of an all too common human experience, points us to another unseen dimension to our lives. One which is fundamental to Christianity and is one which gives us the assurance that, no matter how precarious and forbidding the prospect of travelling may seem, there is a meaning and a destination to all our Christian journeying.

Loneliness can often be the price we pay for love. Recent social trends would seem to suggest that people are marrying later in life as the search for work and career pursuits take precedence. The struggle to attain financial security in an increasingly expensive, competitive world often wins out over the desire to commit to and settle down in a lasting relationship. More and more people in the United Kingdom find themselves living alone, and the statistics aren't helped by the fact that divorce has also increased exponentially since as far back as the 1960's. In a society where families are increasingly fragmented, parents and especially grandparents, often find themselves isolated from their families. This may be the era of Twitter, Facebook, Skype and emails, but somehow an increased ability to communicate seems directly proportional to people's inability to form significant, lasting relationships.

Although there is a myriad of ways to keep in touch, it might be argued that those very things have helped to disempower us from establishing a real connection with each other, through a common culture of shared meanings, ideals, and hopes and fears.

One of the greatest challenges I faced when I became a university chaplain was being plunged into an environment that was almost completely secular in its composition and outlook. As one of the so-called 'new' universities, Anglia Ruskin had no church, no gathered Christian community, and scarcely any experience of a formal Chaplaincy in its midst. It was just a community of thousands of students and staff scurrying between offices and lectures, focussed intently on education and the prizes it promised. As a university chaplain, I found that loneliness was among the chief causes of student stress. Leaving home for the first time, an inability to make friends, and feelings of academic inadequacy in comparison with one's peers, all contributed to a feeling of isolation.

Chaplaincy found itself occupying the ground floor of a student accommodation block on the University's new Rivermead Campus, and a kitchen-diner and four empty student bedrooms became the Chaplaincy Centre. One of the challenges was to create a social space so that the Chaplaincy might be able to conduct a ministry of hospitality and welcome. At the beginning of the autumn semester, when the bulk of new students arrived, the Chaplaincy Centre would put on a series of welcome meals on campus. The kitchen-diner had been carefully arranged to feel as much like the welcoming/receiving room of a private house as possible and not like a refectory or dining hall. During one of these welcome meals (pizzas if I recall correctly) a German student who had been standing by herself in the corner suddenly burst into tears. Alarmed that it might be my cooking, I quickly sought to ascertain the cause of her distress. She told me that the room, with all the new students eating together, forcefully reminded her of her kitchen at home; which was a large room, important to the family, where a lot of time had been spent together, sharing food and company. Suddenly she had been confronted with a powerful memory of love and security, which was now the cause of her homesickness, and also her shyness and reticence about trying to make new friends.

On My Own...

I believe that our God might be a shy and a lonely God. There are those who would argue that God is, in himself, Love and has no need of our companionship, worship or existence. But I believe the opposite is true; that *because* God is love, he is constantly, creatively and sacrificially giving of himself. Yet because in love, he doesn't impose himself, the scriptures frequently present him as almost shy; they are a catalogue of direct and personal contact between God and the individuals singled out to help carry forward his will and direction for his people. I have always marvelled at the apparent timidity and vulnerability of God's approach and the huge gamble played by God, that human beings might ever hear and answer his call in the first place.

Shyness and loneliness might not seem to be very God-like attributes, but they are useful concepts to help us understand the nature of God's relationships with his people, which underscores a lot of scripture. God's loneliness - his separation from the people he loves - is written into Creation's story. When God is walking in his newly created garden during the cool of the day he calls out to Adam and Eve, a father wanting to be with his beloved son and daughter to share with them the delights of companionship. But instead, the result of that meeting is a terrible separation as the truth comes out about his children's temptation and disobedience.

The story of Moses and the burning bush is one that reveals God's shyness and loneliness. His grief at the suffering and enslavement of his people is evidenced when he tells Moses that he has heard his people's cry and wants to return to be by their side and lead them to safety. However, first he has to attract Moses' attention. Like a timid, yet curious child who wants to play with his friends but is wary of effecting an introduction or an adult that needs help but who is too shy and reluctant to ask for it, God mediates his awesome presence in a bush that is on fire but does not seem to be consumed in the flames. It is a message in a bottle, a message thrown out in the hope that Moses' curiosity might prevail, and that he might find the bottle and the message it contains. 'When the Lord saw that he had turned aside to see, God called to him out of the bush, "Moses! Moses!"'[Exodus 3:1-6] How easily one of the greatest, world changing conversations between the creator and his created might never have happened!

The ensuing relationship between God and his people reveals a litany of shyness borne of that separation and a realisation that for human beings to grow they need guidance, but not control. They need to be free to live, to learn, to suffer, to die, and those fragile, vulnerable messages in bottles to the people he loves, can best be thrown to those whose own fragility and vulnerability make them ideal for the task. At the dead of night, the call comes to Samuel, a mere strip of a boy, and also the selection of the greatest King that Israel will ever see has a very shaky beginning. It is David, but he cannot possibly be *the one* because he is the youngest son of the household of Jesse the Bethlehemite, also his job is minding the sheep. Moses' incredulity that God wants him is based on the fact that he has, 'Never been eloquent…I am slow of speech and slow of tongue', and it takes repeated assurances from God that he will be given what to say and taught how to say it. The only consolation for this enormous task is the assurance given to all of us; that the desire of God to walk hand in hand with women and men in the garden of the world remains undimmed.

From within a burning bush, in the dead of night, at the entrance to a cave, God commonly chooses to speak to his beloved; not through earthquake wind and fire but through a gentle whisper. And the Incarnation is the most graphic example of that phenomenon, although it is of course the end of God's shyness, his diffidence, his caution. He now grows himself as a human being and there is now no longer any need for intermediaries for God to be able to attract the attention of humankind. More than calling us in the night, visiting us in the guise of a stranger, or asking us to look at the elements to discern his presence - that he might perceive us from the outside looking in - now God literally jumps into our skin. He inhabits humanity and a new relationship with his people, confirmed forever by Gabriel's message to Mary, beginning instead from the inside out.

However, it is not the end of God's loneliness. Father and Son are identified separately in the Gospels, God describes Jesus as his child, precious beyond words. 'This is my beloved Son', is a phrase repeated more than once. The prospect of Jesus' death being only moments away is an ever present reality; from Herod's slaughter of innocent children in his attempt to do away with the Infant King; to an outraged mob who hustle him to the edge of the cliff with the intention of throwing him off; to being a target for stoning as a result of the righteous indignation of the Jews infuriated by his claim to be the Messiah. He who once declared his identity to Moses through a burning bush, now does so again but face to face with his accusers, in a tense conversation reported in St. John's Gospel which culminates in the dramatic declaration, 'Before Abraham was, I am'. [John 8: 39-59] Yet like all parents, God knows the pain and anxiety of loving but having to let go; Jesus has to be free to live, to learn, to suffer, and to die. Consequently with the life of God on earth there is *still* the timidity and vulnerability of it all - the lonely, agonised watching and waiting of a father who cannot, and must not interfere, but who sees from a distance the capricious fortune that true freedom entails.

Despite the fact that Jesus is often surrounded by lots of people and noise and activity, it is easy to pick up the sense that he was nevertheless alone; but then aloneness wasn't the issue. The Gospels testify to Jesus' desire to be alone, rising early in the morning, or going to an isolated place late in the evening to seek his Father's guidance and to pray. In Christ's ministry, especially of course in his Passion, it was loneliness that was the *real* protagonist. Aloneness is something that can be chosen, but loneliness is generally something that is imposed. When Jesus is finally handed over to his captors in Gethsemane he experiences, through a meek passivity, the world's power to ignore his needs and do him the harm that was identified earlier, and loneliness would have been a terrifying by-product of that powerlessness. His closest friends desert him, his unforgiving enemies surround him to commit verbal and physical abuse, but perhaps worst of all, he experiences the grief of a Son's loneliness when apparently abandoned by his Father.

He who had sustained his Son through all those years of aloneness, at this final hour, now seemed conspicuous by his absence. The silence of God, his heavenly Father, at this terrible moment is the result of the decision taken within the heart of the Trinity and described by St. Paul in his letter to the Philippians, that entailed God having, 'Emptied himself, taking the form of a slave... and being found in human form... became obedient to the point of death'. [Philippians 2: 7-8] The shout of 'Eloi Eloi Lema Sabachthani' from the cross is a cry of anger and desolation at utter parental abandonment, and it is the most powerful testimony to divine loneliness that we have. Father where are you? What have I done? Why have you abandoned me? [Mark 15: 33-34]

When I was young, I used to think that when it rained and the sky became black God was upset and was crying. Although of course when one grows up, one puts away childish things, something of that infantile picture of God remains in my subconscious. I can't help thinking, prior to the ninth hour when Jesus' last act on the cross was to bow his head and give up his spirit, that the darkness which came over the land for three hours; and the tearing of the Temple curtain from top to bottom; and the earthquake which split the rocks and the tombs; whatever other significance they may have, they are powerful symbols of an angry, grieving, frustrated, outraged father who cannot do anything other than strike his fist against a wall. God may have loved the world so much that he sent his only Son, but it cost him dearly too - because to free the world, he had to let his only Son be free.

On the Brink...

It was mentioned earlier that the whole concept of being misunderstood in life played a large part in the complex web of reasons why Jesus went to the cross. The cross represents the antithesis of forgiveness and compassion, a challenge to the man and his message, which goes beyond a denial of his authority and into the attempted destruction of his identity and purpose, the most serious theft of what 'belongs' to a person that can ever be perpetrated. From the perspective of those responsible for Jesus' death, the story of the crucifixion is not about turning the other cheek or loving your enemies. It is the ultimate example of an action that belongs to the old dispensation that advocated an eye for an eye, a tooth for a tooth, and it is this that made the loneliness of Jesus complete.

We would like to think that something we did or something we left to the world endures after our lives are over. So that we could feel there was, after all this, some reason for us having lived on the earth. But the crucifixion of Jesus was also about putting to death what Jesus *did,* his 'good works' of healing, delivering, teaching, and restoring. There would now be no one willing or able to remember, or return the compliment. He who had come to proclaim liberty to captives was now one himself. And the awfulness of the taunt thrown at Jesus as he hung as a prisoner on his cross that, 'He saved others; he cannot save himself', is that it was not just a refusal to accept the miraculous liberty he gave to so many others, but it was a parody of it; goodness turned to evil intent which now could do no more than enforce Jesus' captivity. To be ignored is one thing, to be laughed at is another, and it is mockery, above all else, that helps to ensure an intolerable loneliness.

The concept of the loneliness of God on Good Friday, in all its guises, speaks to us of an aspect of our human experience which we have all shared from time to time. There is a soulful, bereaved dynamic that is going on between Father and Son on Good Friday. This is *still* his beloved son, and it is through a father's grief that we know it will forever be true: despite the necessity of his non-intervention, despite the cruelty, which has now made him almost unrecognisable, despite the abandonment and ridicule which has made him almost unknowable. This speaks to our own experiences of bereavement and loss even if, whilst having to endure those things, any intellectual or emotional link with Christ on his cross may seem elusive.

Parents and guardians who may have felt more grief for us than they were ever able to express or able for us to realise.

Brothers, sisters, companions, and friends who we may feel have never adequately understood or realised our experience of the sense of loss for them, or theirs for us, and which may have remained unsaid and unaccounted for, but, in the despairing silence of the cross on Good Friday, are gathered up into a collective grief which unites all of us, and which can also be located within God's aching heart.

Everything we do and everything we are; from our own births to our joyful and hopeful parents, to the relationships we form, to the children *we* bear in joy and hope, all have a default setting built into them. It is that bereavement, one day, will be the cost of our loving. Fundamentally we are creatures of hope, and love's pursuit, and the all-consuming, never ending human desire to find it and to grow it is proof positive that in the end, love *is* stronger than death. For a while though, for a season in our lives, it renders us castaways, like the man featured in the song by The Police.

In his book 'A Grief Observed', reflecting on the imminent death of his wife, C.S. Lewis writes movingly about what it was like to find himself standing at this crossroads; faced with a love that could still bring him happiness, but which was also about to break his heart.

> "It is incredible how much happiness, even how much gaity, we sometimes had together after all hope was gone. How long, how tranquilly, how nourishingly we talked together that last night!
>
> And yet, not quite together. There's a limit to 'one flesh'. You can't really share someone else's weakness, or fear, or pain. What you feel may be bad. It might conceivably be as bad as what the other felt, though I should distrust anyone who claimed it was. But it

would still be quite different…

We both knew this. I had my miseries, not hers. She had hers, not mine. The end of hers would be the coming of age of mine. We were setting out on different roads. This cold truth, this terrible traffic regulation - ('You, madam, to the right - you, sir, to the left') is just the beginning of the separation which is death itself." [7]

To grapple with the concept of God's loneliness through the events of Good Friday enables us to locate our own loneliness - those dark times of depression and non-comprehension - within a divine companionship and understanding borne of the suffering that was *his*.

The loneliness of Jesus though is that of the long distance runner, someone who is marked out and identified as the *only* one equipped to run the race to acquire our salvation. In the last chapter a verse from 'There is a Green Hill Far Away' was highlighted that spoke of there being 'No other good enough' to run that race, that it was 'He only' who could open the gate of Heaven to all believers. Despite my discomfort identified with the expression of those sentiments, they nevertheless offer something relevant to our current debate; on our Christian journeys part of the loneliness which can afflict us, lies in a requirement to assume responsibility and a self-sacrifice that lies uniquely within our identity as servants of Jesus Christ.

We may rejoice at the true colours of the woman cured of her haemorrhaging, who was called out from the crowd to declare herself as the toucher of the hem of Jesus' robe, to be held up as an example of what can be done for one of faith. Or those of Zacchaeus the tax collector, who when called down from the tree in which he was hiding, so that the amazing inclusiveness of Christ's call could be seen, declared his repentance and restitution for all he had defrauded. To be 'exposed' in this way, whether it is about the revealing of the truth that defines you, or the goodness to which you are called and which you are truly capable, can be a lonely and isolating process, often resulting in persecution and ridicule. Not only because it marks you out but because it can convince others of the need for the truth to be declared about themselves.

When Jesus taught his disciples the Lord's Prayer, it was the uniqueness of that prayer which continues to identify, unite, and equip Christians for the often difficult and demanding identification of their 'true colours' as they undertake their journeys of faith. The structure of the prayer he gave them was specific; a recognition of God's presence and power first, *then* a request for things we need to get us through life and to make it more tolerable. But for most of us, our desires, anxieties, and needs are powerful drivers dominating the way we live. Encouraged as we are to pray, and with a belief that God will hear and have compassion on all the things we place before him and for that I am sure there is rejoicing in heaven, when we say the Lord's Prayer the request, 'Give us this day our daily bread' finds its way to heaven's door first!

Looking through the daily sheaf of prayer requests left on a prayer board situated in Chelmsford Cathedral, ones that say, 'Hallowed be your name', are comparatively rare. Each of them addresses a specific, unique personal or family situation and over the course of a year they amount to the prayers of thousands of different people. Most of them seem unaware of the others' presence and concerns, yet each has a pervading sense of loneliness, and are united by the common desire that God do something to comfort and reassure them. The song by The Police pictures billions of bottles littering the shoreline, each enclosing the message within from its fellows, but all of them looking for a home and an end to loneliness; all of them despatched with the same urgency, hope, and expectation. As R.S.Thomas describes it, 'Prayers like gravel, flung at the sky's window, hoping to attract the loved one's attention'.[8]

In the University Chaplaincy Centre mentioned earlier, two of the former bedrooms became a large lounge with the aid of the disposal of a party wall. This doubled as the worship space, and the challenge was, how to create a spiritual focus that wouldn't compromise the multi-faith nature of the campus or put off those who would find it a comfortable, safe space where they could sit. The solution, placed as a focal point in the room, was a curved 'wall' of house bricks, situated so that there were gaps between them; with an invitation to leave a card with a prayer intention or request in the wall which would be picked up at daily prayer. I was astonished by how many used the prayer wall and also by the intense and often heart rending tales they had to tell: people who may never have dreamed of making a formal approach to Chaplaincy, but who responded to the opportunity for anonymity and the knowledge that someone, somewhere, would pray for them and with them. The hundreds of prayer requests made over the years reminded me of the messages in bottles sung about by The Police, left in the hope that someone would find them and act upon them.

For those of us whose prayers of intercession, for ourselves and others, are so often filtered through a prism of loneliness borne of a burden of care, an endurance of persecution or ridicule, or dictated by a desperate need, many uttered out of a sense of powerlessness to affect or change events, it is possible to see in the billions of messages launched, a symmetry with the prayers of Jesus in Gethsemane and on the cross. Fired by this intolerable loneliness, a request for daily bread in its many forms finally yields to 'Hallowed be your name' and finds resolution in 'Your will be done'.

On the cross there is intercessory prayer for others; those who are perpetrating the violence who do not know what they are doing, whose ignorance forms the wellspring for the request for their forgiveness. This is closely followed by an angry, despairing cry for help to a heavenly Father who is conspicuous by his absence, and perhaps most easily of all this helps us to ground our experience of prayer in the wood of the cross. Then after the exhaustion of all other desires, anxieties, and needs, when in a moment that is both heartbreaking and life mending, at the intersection of pain and love, and the one thing that matters most is to let ourselves be cradled by a God who is well acquainted with grief. 'Father into your hands I commend my spirit'.

As the clouds gather, and the onlookers scoff, and God grieves, and Christ despairs, and evil is at the height of its power, the cross itself becomes a 'message in a bottle'. The hope of salvation is not lost, but as the waves appear to swamp the boat, something life affirming in this awful and destructive event is not annihilated but will live to be discovered another day: a message washed up on the shore of the resurrection, eventually retrieved from inside the tomb and delivered to Mary Magdalene and the women who have come to grieve: 'He is not here: but has risen'.

Finally, here is 'Hallowed be your name'. This is a recognition that confused by events, plunged into darkness, blinded by pain, and isolated by loneliness though we may be, the last despairing prayerful act is to fall into the hands of the living, suffering God. A message in a bottle thrown in the hope that somehow, somewhere, someday, he will respond compassionately to our plight. So the billions of bottles, each unique in the nuanced expressions of loneliness they contain, are all enveloped by the shadow of Jesus 'prayers during his suffering hours. And *because* there is divine companionship with our loneliness and suffering, with the prayers that we make and send, we *can* truly say, that we are not alone in being alone.

Strength Through Hope...

We all like happy endings and after the emotional roller coaster which is Holy Week, it is tempting to see Easter Sunday as such, a happy ending, a relief that it has all come right in the end and so, it's 'apologies for the temporary disruption we now resume business as usual'. But Easter Sunday and the victory of the cross is very far from that, the resurrection stories make it clear that there is still much doubt, confusion and pain; and the 'loss' of Jesus the loved one, at the Ascension, in its own way must have been just as painful as was his 'loss' on Good Friday. They had been given back someone they loved, only to have him snatched away from them again. In the Easter Garden love had started to mend lives and on the Ascension Mount love was once again to break hearts. Yes, of course, there was Pentecost and with it a realisation of how Jesus' promise to be with them always would become possible; and yet these twelve disciples who had become Apostles, would always grieve for the Christ they had known in flesh and blood.

In the aftermath of the Crucifixion, when by earthly standards all that Jesus had promised and aspired to had appeared to come to nothing, it is remarkable that despite everything Jesus' disciples appear to have stuck together. In the Garden of Gethsemane we are told that all the disciples abandoned Jesus and fled for their lives, but some of the resurrection stories make it clear that at least the majority of them continued to meet. At the tomb, Mary Magdalene is told to go to the brothers and give them the Good News of the Resurrection, which implies that she would know where to find them. Also when Jesus appears to them, even though on the first occasion Thomas is not with them, it is clear that the disciples are together albeit, 'The doors of the house where the disciples had met were locked for fear of the Jews' [John 20: 11-29]. Each would have had their own unique memories of friendship, forsaking, and betrayal, but at this point what bound them together was precisely that 'shared uniqueness'; pieces of a jigsaw puzzle that needed to be fitted together and shared.

That is why Jesus chose a meal as the primary event in which to recall his presence with his church. Apart from the immense theological and religious significance of choosing Passover to usher in the new and final act of God's salvation, the bread and wine would have called the disciples back as closely as possible to the physical presence and love of Jesus Christ. When the Early Church faced repeated dangers and persecutions, I am sure it was the memory of a warm, intimate occasion spent reclining in Jesus' company - enjoying the Passover food and drink - and being the beneficiaries of that act of tender service normally administered by the lowliest servant, as much as it was obedience to the command, "Do this in remembrance of me", that would have been their inspiration and strength through difficult, dark, and dangerous times. For us who, unlike Thomas, are the ones blessed because we have *not* seen yet believed, the Eucharist takes us back to a time of intense closeness in the Upper Room that was identified earlier. The bread and wine are not merely symbols of Christ's suffering and death, but remembrances too of a time when the lover and the beloved were together, both in love and in grief.

Love bade me welcome; yet my soul drew back,

   Guilty of dust and sin.

But quick-eyed Love, observing me grow slack

> *From my first entrance in,*
> *Drew nearer to me, sweetly questioning*
> *If I lacked anything.*
>
> *'A guest,' I answer'd, 'worthy to be here':*
> *Love said, 'You shall be he.'*
> *'I, the unkind, ungrateful? Ah, my dear,*
> *I cannot look on Thee.'*
> *Love took my hand and smiling, did reply,*
> *'Who made the eyes but I?'*
>
> *'Truth, Lord: but I have marr'd them: let my shame*
> *Go where it doth deserve.'*
> *'And know you not,' says Love, 'Who bore the blame?'*
> *'My dear, then I will serve.'*
> *'You must sit down,' says Love, 'and taste my meat.'*
> *So I did sit and eat.* [9]

This is George Herbert's famous poem 'Love'. It portrays an unequivocal invitation to the sinner to enjoy the tenderness and embrace of the Eucharist, the Holy Communion. But the sinner draws back, reluctant to respond because, 'guilty of dust and sin', 'I, the unkind, ungrateful? Ah, my dear, I cannot look on Thee'. But quick-eyed love is insistent; God the creator and redeemer has done his work, and a place at the table awaits. The sinner responds instinctively with a pledge to action, 'My dear, then I will serve'. However, what is required is not doing, but being; a reminder that sharing the Gospel begins not by trying to communicate it to another, but by first acknowledging that it has happened to you. Herbert's use of the imperative in the last two lines of the poem and the graphic, stark reference to the physical experience of eating food - which places the sharing of the bread and wine as absolutely central to this process - is striking. "'You must sit down', says Love, 'and taste my meat'. So I did sit and eat.'"

The poem helps us to visualise that it is within the context of the sharing of Holy Communion when we realise the truth, that it is here where we experience a love which restores but which has yet to be fulfilled. If we allow the Eucharist to immerse us in the physical presence of Jesus Christ, and to identify us and link us in the most literal, graphic way possible to the warmth and the love of that Last Supper, we get a glimpse of glory that tantalises us, teases us like a God who hides in a burning bush, or speaks in a small voice, which will one day be ours to fully possess and to enjoy. 'For now we see in a mirror dimly' says St. Paul, 'but then we will see face to face. Now I know only in part; then I will know fully, even as I have been fully known'. [1 Corinthians 13:12] Every time we taste those painful, love filled fruits of the Kingdom, the belief that all this will one day be a reality and that our loneliness *will* be at an end is, indeed, the hope that will keep us together.

Until that day, a taste and a glimpse is all we get, overshadowed as we are by the perpetual identification of bread and wine as symbols of suffering, of the absence of God, of the consequences of misunderstanding and betrayal; but also they are reminders that Good Friday is the ultimate example of that new commandment Jesus gave to his disciples to love one another. New, because it overturned thousands of years of a genetic predisposition to kill or be killed - to claim an-eye-for-an-eye and a tooth-for-a-tooth - and which finds its fulfilment in the words, 'Father, forgive'.

It is a divine companionship between our loneliness and suffering with God's own on the cross which can be expressed both through the *call to love* - generously, riskily, and sacrificially - and to locate and define that vocation and its enormous potential for loneliness within the *sharing of Holy Communion*. Buoyed up by this divine companionship with God's own loneliness and grief, and its prayerful expression on the cross, and reflections of the fact that the graphic, physical reminders of Good Friday each time we experience Holy Communion, give us strength and hope for our Christian journeys. We are given a glimpse of the promised reunion to come, and we are reminded of the time when Jesus said that people will journey from East and West and North and South and sit at table in the Kingdom of God. Like billions of bottles with their messages all washed up on the same shore; people hitherto unknown, each with their unique claim to loneliness, are brought together by their common desire to communicate and to be heard. It is a vision of the things still to come, and its beginning is with the cross of Jesus Christ.

IVOR MOODY
Songs for
the Soul
•
4

Blowin' in the Wind

Encountering Reconciliation

In 1962 Bob Dylan wrote a song called 'Blowin' in the
Wind'. The song is built around a series of questions piled one
on top of another. It yearns for a time when war and hatred will
be no more. The frequency and savagery of acts of violence
and neglect which currently beset the world are highlighted by
a demand to know how many times; how many years; and how
many deaths? It is an impatient song that is a lament for peace
for a world that seems sunk in violence and despair. The song
exudes a frustration, not only that humankind seems unable to
see a hoped for and hope filled future, but that a lack of vision
is also responsible for the inability to conduct relations in the
here and now, which might mimic or anticipate a hoped for,
hoped filled future.

The song, like Nina Simone's 'Don't Let Me Be Misunderstood',
is set amidst the racial unrest in Dylan's home country of the

United States. The song has been described as an anthem of the 1960's Civil Rights Movement. And one that encapsulated the hope and despair of black people in the USA who were fighting for recognition and equality, a campaign driven by the famous civil rights leader Martin Luther King Jr. In fact, the song was sung on the steps of the Lincoln Memorial in 1963 a few hours before King delivered his famous, 'I have a dream' speech.

One of the difficulties about undertaking the Christian journey of faith, is that our prayers for peace and justice in the world seem to fall on stony ground, but the answer to Dylan's questions - and ours - are 'Blowin' in the Wind', a phrase which punctuates the entire song. One might understand this in many ways, but it could be interpreted as a metaphor that as the wind swirls around and between us, and is to be found in the midst of us, none of us has to look far for the solution to the sad conundrums posed by Dylan's song. An end to violence is within the capability and grasp of all of us to achieve, if only there was the will and the humility to do so. It is also, 'in the wind', that all of our attempts at peace and reconciliation will one day be consummated by God's final action to deal, once and for all, with the causes and unrepentant perpetrators of violence and so establish a kingdom of peace without end.

If that deceptive word, 'misunderstanding', hides under its innocent, unassuming exterior a torrent of abuses which helped to send Christ to his cross, then another such word is 'goodness'. Jesus himself was uneasy about the concept of goodness. When a rich young ruler, as Luke called him, addressed him as 'Good Teacher', he was chastised by Jesus for using the description 'Good'; it was something that could be applied to God alone. This was not a denial of Jesus' sanctity, but a warning that 'goodness' was not to be used as flattery to win favour or to get what was desired.

We need to start by realising that goodness is a loaded word. The Western world has been nurtured on the unshakable belief that freedom and democracy is good and right. It is a way of life that seems to promise personal autonomy, choice, and a materialistically comfortable existence, all of which engenders feelings that, with such qualities, we fairly and squarely inhabit the moral high ground. However, the pursuit of 'goodness' has a bloody history.

We are children of modernity and a secularism borne of a faith in reason and science, which has convinced us that our way of doing things is right. This should make us feel uncomfortable, because all too often what we consider 'good' and 'bad' can cause us to erect new and oppressive boundaries; these can mask our ability to detect the exclusionary tendencies that emerge in our own judgements and practices. As we have seen, 'Holocaust', 'Apartheid', and 'Ethnic Cleansing', are all twentieth-century words which testify what happens when the pursuit of what is thought to be good, right or acceptable reaches extreme proportions. The frightening thing about this pursuit of 'goodness', is that evil no longer has to have a supernatural identity. It can sit quite happily in the bosom of human behaviour that thinks evil to be good, and that is true of the behaviour of nation states much as it is of the behaviour of individuals.

In John Milton's epic poem 'Paradise Lost', Satan, one of the three central characters of the drama muses, '*The mind is its own place and in itself, Can make a Heav'n of Hell, a Hell of Heav'n*'. Like the rich young man in the story from St. Luke, people's concept of goodness clashed headlong with the messages and demands of the Gospel. One defined by an adherence to rules and regulations and the other, that goodness was the possession of no one but something which was to be perceived as a 'gift'. More than anything this revealed itself in the conflict about the Sabbath; 'goodness' for the religious leaders was how well a Jew obeyed the law and did no work on this day. 'Goodness' for Jesus was how God could use this day to release people from their burdens and convince them of their preciousness in God's sight.

Which Way...?

One of the most famous parables Jesus told, was about a prodigal son who leaves the family home to live the high life, but who learns the painful lesson that 'home is where the heart is'. It is a wonderful story which can be found in Luke 15:11-32.

In the story, the moral categories and constructs employed by the elder brother concerning his younger brother's departure lies along the axis of bad and good behaviour. Depending on whether or not a rule has been transgressed, determines whether or not you are included or excluded. The mantra of the elder sibling is how he has been 'good' - working like a slave for his father for many years - and therefore condemns the younger brother as 'bad', he tells his father that he has, 'devoured your property with prostitutes'.

We find it difficult not to be sympathetic with this position because we are submerged in a world of fixed rules and retributive justice; amidst relationships which are defined by a morality which regulates acceptance and rejection. This concept of justice sees human beings simply as all worthy of equal treatment by virtue of their common humanity. It is significant that the parable of the prodigal son does not have a happy ending. Despite the pleading of his father, the elder son refuses to join the party thrown for the homecoming of his wayward brother and there the story ends.

The parable of the prodigal son is not about rules and morals dictating the nature of our relationships, it is precisely the other way around. That is not to say that morals and rules are not important; a central point in the telling of the story by Jesus was to assert the proper place of repentance, confession, and the consequences of one's actions; but the priority of relationship supersedes any moral rules, which may be regarded as the arbiter of what should be accepted and what should be rejected.

The sensible logic of the elder brother in the parable, which argues that he is justified in his feelings and reactions to his brother's return and reception is persuasive; we can empathise with him because he feels that an injustice has been done to him. His complaint about his father's behaviour and attitude towards his errant offspring is symptomatic of a complaint that we have all voiced against God from time to time; as we go on our Christian journeys, it is one of the hardest things to manage and to comprehend. Looking back over my priestly ministry, various people whom I have had the privilege of serving and getting to know remain vividly in my memory, because they have conducted a journey of faith accompanied by the most incredible burdens of loss, abuse, prejudice, and unfulfilled desire. Their struggle to keep walking the Emmaus Road is evidenced in the frequently asked question: if God is good and benevolent, why does he permit bad things to happen and bad people to flourish?

It is that very question that permeates the scriptures. In the face of continual violence, persecution, poverty, and the perceived absence of God to hear and grant his people's petitions for safety and restitution, the anguished cry of the psalmist resonates through the generations and echoes the impatient questioning of Dylan's song: 'Will you be angry with us forever? Will you prolong your anger to all generations? Will you not revive us again, so that your people may rejoice in you?' [Psalm 85:4-7]

If we are submerged in a world of fixed rules and retributive justice, then everything within us cries out against a God who might ever overlook the suffering of the victims of violence in favour of the perpetrators of it. In the Old Testament, the Book of Lamentations, written against the backdrop of the catastrophic fall of Jerusalem, the plundering of the Temple in 597 B.C., and the exile into Babylon, is a cry to God about the desolation of its people and the triumph of its foes and tormentors. The heart rending description of the fall of Jerusalem and with all the resulting suffering and hardship leads the poet (and the reader) to ask the question, 'Why'? [Lamentations 5:19-22]

What makes the forgiveness by the father of his wayward son hard to stomach is that the elder son tells us the truth about his years of faithful service. About how he is now forced to reconcile that painful division which has opened up between his filial devotion to his father and the impossible task his father sets him to forgive his brother - even worse, to understand and to reconcile his father's actions. The elder son is faced with a dilemma, which will be familiar to many others who are called to a life of service and devotion to their heavenly Father but find that there is often a painful and expensive cost to that loving.

The painful division which goes to Jeremiah's heart is in the message he delivers. He is torn between an intense love for his people and the necessity, the compulsion, to pronounce God's judgement on their apostasy. It is hard not to equate deeply with the psychological torment of Jeremiah as he cries:

For whenever I speak, I must cry out, I must shout, "Violence and destruction!" For the word of the Lord has become for me a reproach and derision all day long. If I say, "I will not mention him, or speak any more in his name", then within me there is something like a burning fire shut up in my bones; I am weary with holding it in, and I cannot.' [Jeremiah 20:8-9]

The exchange between the elder son and his father, while indoors the party rages for his younger sibling, contrasts the irritable, frustrated impatience of youth with the gentle wisdom of senior years. The patience of the father is seen in the fact that, despite his son's rage at what has happened, the father spends some time gently pleading with his son to come inside and join the party, eventually declaring to him that, 'All that is mine is yours'. The father's patience is the key to the whole story.

The detail Luke gives in his recounting of the parable is significant; the fact that the father recognised his younger son 'while he was still far off'. One can imagine that every morning when the father left the house, he would cast his eyes into the distance, patiently waiting and hoping for his son's return. Then one day a lonely figure appears on the horizon. He is trudging down the road with his head bowed and because of the bond between parent and child, long before the father can see the whites of his eyes, he *knows* that this is his son and runs to meet him. In one of the most memorable and touching moments in the Gospels, Luke tells us, 'He ran and put his arms around him and kissed him'. The father literally hugs his son back into his life. The father of the prodigal son scans the road leading into the far hills each morning looking for the return of his beloved offspring - Jesus gives no clue as to how long he was away - except in the passionate, dramatic embrace between father and son upon the latter's return and the noisy party that ensues. Could it be that the measure of the father's joy is directly proportional to the distance in time that the son had been away?

The son begins his rehearsed speech, 'Father I have sinned against heaven and before you', but it is ignored! The decision to return home is penitence enough, and in the embrace of the father there is no expectation of reparation; no impatient demand to account for lost time; no recrimination about the worry and grief that has been caused; just the sheer joy of the reward of patience that one day, 'This son of mine was dead and has come to life; he was lost and has been found'. The older brother's anger is not to be understood simply in terms of what he perceived was the favouritism of his younger brother, who deserved nothing but instead received the attention he felt *he* deserved, but because it appeared that the father had chosen not to remember the profligacy and dissolute lifestyle which had finally brought his brother to his knees. Any memory of that had been obliterated in the embrace of a father and his son who had *always* been precious and beyond compare, and who was lost but now found. Nothing less can explain the unrestrained joy the father shows upon his youngest son's return.

In contrast to the specific memories of both sons brought to play in the story, is the one who rehearses his set piece of penitential words to speak before his father and the elder son, who wastes no time in reminding his father of the younger brother's waywardness by listing all of his misdemeanours. However the father sweeps all that away, 'Quickly, bring out a robe - the best one - and put it on him; put a ring on his finger and sandals on his feet....' No matter how bad things have become, a father's love and compassion for his son help-lessly overflows; like a dam that can no longer restrain its contents, it bursts forth like a torrent. The father's forgive-ness is not regulated by his children's behaviour and because of that, the father's love remains, immovable and inviolable even after his elder son persists in his rejection of the call to healing and reconciliation.

How Often...?

The tolerant, if painful, patience that God has with suffering and its causes preoccupies a lot of Jesus' teachings. To an angry owner of a barren fig tree, who has come for three years and found no fruit on the tree, it is the gardener who persuades him to not have it cut down but to try again just one more time, 'Sir, let it alone for one more year, until I dig round it and put manure on it'. [Luke 13:6-9]

The parable of the wicked tenants directs our eyes to the crucifixion; to Jesus as the last, and the most important, as the son and heir in a long line of servants and slaves sent by the vineyard owner to collect his produce, who is killed and flung out of the vineyard by those who have possessed it and who seek the sole rights of ownership. And yet the story is also about the patience of God, who displays seemingly endless faith that one day one of his emissaries, albeit his only son, will have the desired effect - repentance and justice will ensue and the vineyard owner will receive his rightful remuneration. The parable is a potted pictorial history of thousands of years of Israelite failure to live in covenant relationship with God, and that has seen countless prophets lose their lives fighting for Yahweh's cause. 'They will respect my son', is the confident expression of the endless hopefulness of God. [Matthew 21:33-45]

What has been described here is a counter-cultural way of loving, which challenges our human, two-dimensional views of what love and goodness really is; and it is the love of the cross. There is a direct relationship between the assumed and accepted 'goodness' of Jesus' enemies and their direct responsibility for ensuring his death. The crucifixion was because his rejection of their notion of good was considered as evil. There was no room for Jesus' version of goodness because the knowledge of what was good was already 'owned' by them, so Jesus had to die.

Earlier I reflected on the vulnerability of a nation that sought to, 'Protect and preserve religious and doctrinal purity in the face of relentless conquest and occupation [which] would have refined and honed the making and despising of outcasts...to preserve and protect national identity'. We know all too painfully from our own lives, and the life of the world around us, that if Jesus truly died 'to make us good', then the project of the crucifixion was a failure. We continue to live in a world which would rather stockpile swords than make ploughshares in its fallen attempts to establish or pursue its goodness and justice. Every minute someone dies as a result of armed violence; every day it is estimated that over twenty thousand children die globally through poverty, hunger, and disease.

In contrast, the open arms of Christ at Golgotha is a sign that God does not want to be a God without humanity, and he is prepared to suffer humanity's violence in order to embrace it. The gesture of an embrace; whether it's lying side by side, arms outstretched wide, or merely a finger enclosing a finger, is an invitation for someone who is familiar and who needs no formal introduction to come close. If so, then the nature of an embrace implies the necessity for patience, for waiting on the other to respond. An embrace is not a grasp for affection, it is an invitation to be loved. As such it is a gesture that entails self-sacrifice, a putting of oneself at the disposal of the other for acceptance or rejection.

Although Jesus was sometimes impatient that people should grasp the depth of God's love for them, and grasp the Gospel imperative that love and forgiveness is stronger than hate and revenge - an impatience that was often fuelled by an anger that helpless people suffer and their tormentors go free - the root of his impatience was the *patience* of the cross. It is the ultimate act of non-violence which met head on a savage act of impatience; that this dangerous, troublesome Jew be silenced once and for all. When Jesus watches those who are driving nails into his hands and feet and drawing lots for his clothing, he does not see a justice which calls for their condemnation, but instead sees the injustice of the ignorance and blindness which keeps them from realising and knowing what they do. This is a scandalous act, not only because it challenges the logic which defines the way we live - an-eye-for-an-eye, a-tooth-for-a-tooth - but also because it challenges us to enshrine this metaphor of *embracing* within our lives.

The Crucifixion was an act of passivity, a gesture of an embrace which echoes the patient wisdom of an old man who hugs his errant son back into his life. Christ's body - fixed eternally in a gesture of embrace - demonstrates an outpouring of love that is *beyond* control, a true 'goodness' predicated not on 'rightness' but on the totality of his self-giving. Yet this is not about the father of a wayward son who features in a story Jesus once told, now the all giving and forgiving parent is Jesus himself, embracing not just one lost sheep but the entire fold.

The embrace of the cross is not only an act of sheer open-ended generosity though, it is also - as Miroslav Volf points out in his book 'Exclusion and Embrace' - a testimony to the ability of God to *forget*. We do not know the crime of the penitent thief who was crucified next to Jesus, we only get insight into the crime of another criminal presented at the drama of the crucifixion, Barabbas. We are told that he had been condemned to death for insurrection and murder. That the thieves crucified with Jesus had committed a crime punishable by death is beyond dispute; part of the penance of the thief who chastises his companion for his taunting of Jesus is, 'We indeed have been condemned justly, for we are getting what we deserve for our deeds, but this man has done nothing wrong'. Jesus' response however takes no account of that; like the father who interrupts his son's speech of repentance with a showering of gifts, the penitent thief is promised paradise for his pains. In a demonstration of forgiveness that is so comprehensive and so all-consuming, whatever crimes that had held sway are now put away, obliterated from any further recall. It is the ultimate demonstration that the divine memory of human beings, as precious beyond compare, is so much more powerful than the memory of their offences. [Luke 23: 39-43]

Our God *needs* to be a forgetting God though, because if redemption is to be the utter, complete, and final thing we need it to be, then it will be unthinkable unless there is, from the heart of Heaven itself, a specific kind of forgetting. Only non-remembering can end the lament over suffering, which no thought can take away and no action can undo. Quite possibly this thought is abhorrent to us, because even if pain and the desire for revenge has gone, the memories still remain. Yet if there could ever be forgiveness for the perpetrators of genocide, the memories of horrors committed in the past are still there to haunt the present generation. If that is the case, then heaven will be incomplete because the lament over suffering will remain. Worse, it will be a kingdom divided against itself:

> "Even re-making the whole world and removing all sources of suffering will not bring redemption if it does not stop incursions of the unredeemed past into the redeemed present through the door of memory.... If heaven cannot rectify Auschwitz, then the memory of Auschwitz must undo the experience of heaven.... either heaven will have no monuments to keep the memory of horror alive, or it will be closer to hell than we would like to think." [10]

Like voices from the grave, the loud insistence of all those whose lives have been sacrificed for the strident perception of the 'goodness' and 'rightness' espoused by others, echo the demands of many campaigners for justice whose insistence that the only right and proper solution to murder is to murder back; an eye for an eye and a tooth for a tooth. We baulk at the prospect that if there is a possibility that forgetting is part of God's redemptive process, there is the monumentally uncomfortable prospect that the Herods, Judas' and Pontius Pilates of this world - providing that repentance is their end game - will one day be dressed in a white robe. Even though it is an image that might be intolerable for us to face, as Volf reminds us, everything we believe about the nature of God and the achievement of the cross requires us to seriously consider it.

How Long...?

All of this might help us to forgive, but does it help us to forget, or do we still have to carry our pain into heaven? For a long time in secondary school, I was bullied by two other boys. It was largely verbal, but its frequency and persistence made it all the more menacing. My memories are that many days at school were filled with fear. I would dread blind corners where I might bump into them, and going to and from school involved constant vigilance. The experience was so traumatic that for years afterwards I harboured a violent grudge against them. I used to dream about the physical violence my alterego would have done to exact revenge against them. To this day I can recall them as if it all happened just yesterday, even more clearly than some of my friends who accompanied me all the way through school! It is only in the last few years that my anger at the legacy they left has truly and completely abated. The memories are still there but the desire for reparation, thankfully, has finally gone cold.

If it has taken me nearly forty years to remember my experience of being bullied at school without psychological pain, then it is inconceivable to me that the monstrous memories of countless acts of murder will *ever* be recalled without hurt and anger. In his song, Dylan asserts that the list of all those who have died violently is far too long. That the spilling of so much blood, and the loss of so much humanity surely means that even the passing of centuries will not snuff out the agonised memories of their loss, but they will be genetically encoded into generation upon generation, passed on until the end of time.

If that is even possible then we need something else, above and beyond our present experience and our painful memories of the past, to help us conceive and understand a future where redemption is total; and the humbled perpetrators of violence and the painful legacies they leave have all been cleansed. Walter Brueggemann describes it as *imagination*. Sometimes the only thing that will lift us from the powerlessness of despair and the feeling that nothing can or will transform the violent hegemony of a world that seems irretrievably set on a path of ultimate self-destruction, is the creation of what he perceives as an alternative reality. Through the exercise of imagination one is able to ditch the comfortable, familiar story in which they have taken refuge and can recount one's life differently - an account that is not afraid to contain the often challenging demands and dimensions of faith.[11]

This is no mere fairytale-like escape from the harsh pressures and realities of that which would enslave us though, but something based firmly on those past, painful, hurtful memories that threaten to cling to us and accompany us into the Kingdom. Now, through imagination and this alternative reality, those memories become not our taskmasters but our servants, being reminders for us of what heaven is *not* but what it could be; what it might feel like, once and for all, to be totally free of pain. If the portrayal of goodness on the cross is a scandal because it exposes all our flawed attempts at 'goodness', then it also offers us a vision of the actual goodness to which we are all called to aspire.

The cross is a reminder not that Jesus died to make us good, but that goodness in its true, divine, and heavenly apparel is part of the vision of the Kingdom of God that keeps us striving in our faith, keeps throwing our prayers to heaven like messages in bottles, and helps us to keep trying to love because we know it's worth the cost. This is why goodness and love have an *eschatological* dimension to them; it is a reminder to us that as Christians, we all live in the tension between the 'now' and the 'not yet'. Perhaps the presence and recall of painful memories, both individual and corporate, are necessary not only to better understand the present but to keep alive a vision of a pain free, tyranny free future - to see the true colours of God's world.

We struggle with the tension between our present and the future which is God's; between what we strive for now and what, through hope, prayer, and Christian service, we believe one day will be fully realised; between our attempts at 'goodness', which only seem to inoculate and increase violence, and the goodness of God, which will one day finally allow people to be truly free. Paul reminds the church in Rome, whose members no doubt would have been fearful and distrusting that persecution would ever bear its promised fruit, that, 'If we hope for what we do not see, we wait for it with patience' [Romans 8:25]. If we do live in that tension between the 'now' and the 'not yet', persuaded to see beyond the pain of the cross to the promise of paradise, then what is required is patient endurance - a stillness and calmness borne of trust in God that, despite the ferment, fire, and failures of life, ultimately all will be well.

Earlier we said that the Eucharist gives us the ultimate sacramental realisation of that very conundrum, and through the bread and wine, 'we get a taste of God, we get a glimpse of glory that tantalises us', but 'until that day, a taste and a glimpse is *all* we get, overshadowed as they are by the perpetual identification of bread and wine also as symbols of suffering....' These are dangerous memories because they are a constant reminder to a world sunk in brutality, violence, and despair that Christians hold on to an ideology to change; to act differently; to show the world a better way, which is a departure from that of the accepted hegemony of the day. They also dare to suggest an answer to all those questions raised in Dylan's song, that one day the vision of Isaiah will be realised that, 'No more shall the sound of weeping be heard.... or the cry of distress. No more shall there be in it an infant that lives but a few days, or an old person who does not live out a lifetime' [Isaiah 65:19-20]. The daring, dangerous prospect that we remember in order that we may forget, and be caught up in that divine forgetfulness which is God's, is made possible by the cross of Christ, the ultimate symbol of what it is to remember and to forget.

If we were to stop here, with an image of redemption that speaks of an embrace from the cross made by a patient and forgetful God, whose notion of justice is dominated by love, then the picture and definition of redemption and the work of the cross offered would be inadequate. Why? Because the cross is not and never has been merely about pure and simple forgiveness. It is also about the world of cruelty and injustice being set right.

There is a costliness to God's patience, both for himself and all the victims of the perpetrators of violence, because every day of patience permits more bloodletting and oppression. Part of the 'deal' struck between the gardener and the furious owner of the barren fig tree is, 'If it bears fruit next year, well and good; but if not, you can cut it down'. The judgement of the wicked tenants pronounced by Jesus at the end of that parable, makes it clear that the longevity of God's compassion and forgiveness is not infinite.

Not to realise this or to skirt around it in our unease and embarrassment, that a God who judges is somehow incompatible with a God who loves and saves, is not only to misunderstand the message of the Good News but worse; to water it down so much that we think of Jesus as nothing more than a harmless, nice man pedalling a toothless, inanimate Gospel. It is also to deny responsibility to give an account of ourselves, to go out and to bear fruit, to double the five talents we have been given. The man who cried with grief at the loss of his friend Lazarus, and reacted compassionately and indignantly to so many that came to him wanting release from years of burdens of pain, suffering and rejection, is the same person whose language and teaching about God's Kingdom is rife with predictions and warnings for those that refuse to repent and believe in the Gospel.

As abhorrent as it might be to even countenance, it is possible that some human beings, even though they are created in God's image, are so sunk in evil practices and intent, so convinced that hate and violence have their own inviolable logic and are the only means to achieve 'goodness', that they have immunised themselves against any acceptance of God's truth and goodness - even though no one lies beyond God's power to change and redeem. Perpetrators of violence who, because they will *never* repent in the face of the Gospel calling them to a love, compassion, and forgiveness which will itself never change, will *never* wear a white robe. So an inseparable part of the vision of a future when God will be all-in-all, must also entail a moment when God will judge, not because He delights in kicking people when they are down, but because there are some that will refuse God's loving, forgiving embrace, and will, without any possibility of diversion, seek to make a hell of heaven.

What are we to say then; that violence has the last word? That the last act of God will be the squashing of his enemies? By no means. It is so that a world can finally exist without injustice, violence, and hatred that these things and the people that perpetrate them, without hope or intention of ever acknowledging and repenting of their progeny of evil, will finally be brought to an end. For those of us who struggle on with our Christian journeys, confronted by evil and violence and called to forgive not seven but seventy seven times, the knowledge of God's reconciliation, and his judgement upon those who heap burdens upon others, gives us the assurance that, however heavy the load we have to carry on our pilgrimage to heaven, it is worth taking the next step, because pain and suffering will not have the final say.

IVOR MOODY
Songs for
the Soul
•
5

The Sounds of Silence

Discovering Power

Originally the song, 'The Sounds of Silence', appeared on an album called 'Wednesday Morning 3am'. The album did not sell well and Simon and Garfunkel went their separate ways. However, the song was rearranged, re-recorded and became an instant hit, bringing the duo back together, propelling them to international stardom, and cementing their status as one of the greatest pop duos of all time.

Although Paul Simon has said that there were no intended deep meanings behind the words, it nevertheless captured the imagination of a generation, coming when it did in 1963, during the aftermath of the assassination of President Kennedy. The song was heard again in September 2011, when Paul Simon sang it accompanied by a lone guitar to the reflective, grieving crowd at Ground Zero on the tenth anniversary of the terrorist destruction of the World Trade Center.

'The Sounds of Silence', speaks of the silence of ignorance with its inability and unwillingness to listen to those who recognise the signs of the times, those who proclaim justice and the need to allow peace room to grow. It is the graffiti artists who leave their messages and warnings by night for the masses to see in the daylight; powerful truths spelled out by powerless people.

Sometimes our Christian journeying is undertaken in the silence borne of a feeling of inadequacy and helplessness, either that our suffering can have any meaning or that our faith can have any impact in the world. But as the song suggests, silence can be a powerful medium of communication. A secular song points to a sacred, prophetic silence which lies at the heart of the Gospels and the experience of Good Friday; one which shapes Jesus' destiny and the achievement of the cross, and one which can inform and sustain our often dark and lonely grappling towards heaven.

The birth of Jesus Christ took place in a land amongst people familiar with oppression and a daily struggle for survival. Despite the cosy image of the birth in a stable in Bethlehem, which often adorns our Christmas cards, the stable is nevertheless a potent symbol of that destitution. It was this experience of poverty and powerlessness - as a Jew living in an occupied land under the heel of a savage oppressor - which did much to shape and develop Jesus' realisation of the powerful message, that the poor and the meek would inherit the earth.

Even before Jesus experienced the weakness and vulnerability of his contemporaries, he embodied that in himself, the result of God emptying himself and taking the form of a servant. His helplessness and vulnerability as a baby is one of the tangible links between the Incarnation and the Crucifixion. That same helplessness and vulnerability is detected then in his fulfilment of Deutero-Isaiah's vision, that our salvation would be procured by one who was wounded for our transgressions and crushed for our iniquities. A silence which surrounds Jesus' suffering, born of an isolation caused by so much hate and misunderstanding, also surrounds his divine birth, which begins not with speech but with silence. 'In the beginning was The Word', proclaims St. John at the start of his Gospel; but because of the Incarnation, 'The Word' assumes the silence and inarticulacy of a new born. He is required to learn speech and the gradual process of discovering his place in the world and what life may hold for him.

So it might not be unreasonable to ask when Jesus came to realise the full meaning and implication of his life and ministry. There has been much theological debate about when Jesus recognised his destiny to be accomplished in Jerusalem. Was he born with the knowledge that he was *always* destined for death, or was that the realisation of something he uncovered little by little as his ministry unfolded?

A Silence That Speaks...

Current sleep science suggests that when we sleep everybody dreams, whether we remember the dreams or not. Dreams are the brain's way of repairing itself, cataloguing and filing all the thoughts, memories, and impressions experienced throughout the day. If this is true, then Jesus must have dreamed too, and if he dreamed then his unconscious self, like ours, would be released from the inhibitions of consciousness, a mind and body in a still, receptive state. Did Jesus have a dream about his destiny on Golgotha's hill, or might it just have been an intellectual and emotional conviction into which he grew? Controversially, it could be argued, that what gives sense and understanding to the immense suffering and sacrifice of Good Friday is the fact that Jesus only became gradually aware of what his glorious destiny was to be, and to assume differently would be to lessen the impact of that suffering and sacrifice.

There is one thing of which we can be reasonably certain; Jesus' periods of inactivity connected intimately with his life of prayer and his perception of what lay in store for him. His times of solitude and retreat from the world, whether it was rest and sleep or emptying the mind to wait upon God, were not infrequently preceded by a time of prayer or a call to decisive action. We said earlier that 'aloneness' was a state Jesus often sought. Mark tells us that Jesus got up in the darkness of the early morning and sought out a lonely place to pray so successfully, that on one occasion when the disciples awoke they couldn't find him, and when they did, they complained that everybody else was looking for him too! [Mark 1:35-37]

In their Gospels, Matthew, Mark, and Luke all place Jesus' sojourn into the wilderness directly before the start of his public ministry and the call of his first disciples. Therefore, they all establish a direct correlation between a perception and a conviction about what Jesus must do, which is garnered through an endurance of silence, borne from a pattern of sleepfulness and wakefulness. Combined with an experience of solitude and an abstinence in his barren, lonely surroundings, this leads to a direct confrontation with that which would divert him from that clarity of purpose and intention.

The relationship between sleeping and waking, which is essential to Jesus' connectivity with his Heavenly Father and nourished in the silence of the wilderness, was to define Jesus' ministry and especially his Crucifixion. Out of this silence and the solitude of the wilderness comes Satan's attack. He is drawn to what he thinks is Christ's vulnerability, the fact that after forty days he is famished and is therefore disorientated and susceptible. What Satan fails to recognise is that the exact opposite is true. The silence of the wilderness has

enabled Jesus to dream, a dream of his identity and his purpose, which would sustain him until the end. In many of the
people's wretched circumstances which Jesus encounters there
is a direct confrontation with evil, a face-to-face contact first
seen in Jesus' experience in the wilderness. It is a confrontation
which finds its denouement with Jesus' arrest, trial, crucifixion,
and that 'opportune time' referred to in Luke's account of the
wilderness temptations, which Satan looks forward to after
his failure to overturn Christ's identity and purpose at the
beginning of his ministry. [Luke 4: 1-13]

Jesus may have been completely alone in the silence of the
wilderness, but in a very real sense he would not have been
lonely. He knew the scriptures so well, that he would have
been aware of the many others before him that had inhabited
and appropriated the dream - the vision - that was now growing in him, each of them, in their own way, signposting Jesus
and us to the cross.

For the young Jesus, sitting in the Temple of Jerusalem
amazing the doctors of the law with his wisdom and understanding, much of the inspiration for his preaching and teaching involved a thorough inhabiting of past heroes of the Jewish
faith. Not only emulating their preaching and teaching but, in
many cases, an understanding of their vocation to serve and
to suffer for righteousness' sake.

Jacob, who after his dream of a ladder reaching up to
Heaven exclaims, 'Surely the Lord is in this place - and I did
not know it!'. Solomon reigns forty years over Israel with the
wisdom granted to him by God in a dream; Elijah fleeing from
his enemies, whose silence through enforced sleep borne of
depression and fear, finds its meaning and significance at the
mouth of a cave in, 'the sound of sheer silence', and the small
voice of God directing him to the next task to be done; the
list goes on and on. These are the silent revelations of those

men and women who not only dreamed of a time like Jesus once told his disciples they were fortunate to see because many before them had longed to see it but could not; but also whose vision of the justice and righteousness of God was shared by Jesus, who came to understand that the cross was the key to its realisation.

It was the spiritual experience of Jesus' predecessors that had such a profound effect upon him, not only in the way he opened himself up to communication with his Heavenly Father, but subsequently in the way he was able to perceive his identity and purpose. It was a process of self-realisation borne of the silence of the wilderness, which proved pivotal to the whole of Jesus' message. In the Synagogue, after his wilderness experiences, Jesus declares himself as the fulfilment of Isaiah's vision that the poor would have the Good News preached to them, and he incurs the wrath of all those who hear him, outraged at the claim Jesus was making [Luke 4:13-30]. It was more than just a common dislike of an upstart that appears to put himself on a pedestal above everyone else. In a tight-knit community whose perception of Jesus was that he shared their powerlessness and oppression, a community which had nurtured and protected him, his desire to be recognised as something different with a message of Good News, which was inclusive of everybody and which would take him away from that community, may well have been seen as an action little short of traitorous. This gives the outraged exclamation of those in the Synagogue on that sabbath day, that this is just the 'carpenter's son', new force and meaning.

Jesus' teaching is shot through with examples of how the powerless, silently and unobserved, have a powerful capacity to shame and to instruct those who wield power in the world. In the story of the 'Widow's Mite', Mark tells us that Jesus purposely sat down opposite from the treasury to watch people making their financial offerings. This is different to Luke's version of the story where Jesus merely looked up, the implication being that he happened to catch the action by being in the right place at the right time. In Mark's version Jesus is watching - a silent activity - and his patience is rewarded by the sight of a poor widow donating two copper coins which, he assures his disciples, is a more generous offering than the others. They had given out of their abundance but, 'She out of her poverty has put in everything she had, all she had to live on'. The phrase, 'everything she had', is an addition to Luke's version, Mark doubly emphasises this woman's poverty [Mark 12: 41-44; Luke 21: 1-4]. What the world would consider an insignificant donation teaches us the true value of a gift, that it arises not from the wallet or purse, but from the heart. Here is a key with which to unlock so much of Jesus' teachings, through the parables he told and the different people and situations he encountered, about what it should be like to be in relationship with God.

A Silence Misunderstood...

If silence, whether perceived in the dreams and aspirations of his ancestors or experienced dramatically in the wilderness, was central to Jesus' understanding of his self-identity and mission, then it is not surprising that silence was also a tool Jesus used to enhance his teachings and to communicate God's love. The Gospels are full of precious silences, making us wonder not only at the chronology and the spaces of Jesus' ministry, but the full impact of what must have passed between him and the people he met. The story of the woman caught in the act of committing adultery and then dragged before Jesus [John 8:1-11], is an example of how Jesus' use of silence ensured the salvation of a sinner, and turned what seemed to be certain death, into another chance to live.

There are two different aspects of silence in this story, and the first is an ominous, threatening one. The writers of Leviticus and Deuteronomy are clear that perpetrators of adultery are deserving of death, 'If a man commits adultery with the wife of his neighbour, both the adulterer and the adulteress shall be put to death' [Leviticus 20:10]. The Pharisees know that they are on rock solid ground and their entrapment of Jesus seems insurmountable. Either Jesus does not uphold the law or he pronounces a death sentence, which would have laid him open to a treasonable charge as only the Roman Governor had the jurisdiction to pronounce the death penalty. Speculation has raged as to why Jesus, rather than giving an instant retort as he usually did, chose instead to be silent and to write - possibly doodle - with his finger in the sand. Due to the conundrum the Pharisees had set him, it is reasonable to surmise that Jesus had to draw a breath; he needed time to think and this silence is a tense, threatening one, because hanging on Jesus' response was whether or not people started throwing stones. It is a wonderfully dramatic moment in the Gospels.

I have already alluded to when Jesus returns to Nazareth to begin his public ministry, and reads from the prophecy of Isaiah in the Synagogue on the Sabbath day. As he rolls up the scroll, gives it back to the attendant, and sits down, Luke tells us of another dangerous, expectant silence when, 'the eyes of all in the Synagogue were fixed upon him'. So here it is not hard to imagine a desire to kill, more powerful than even a thousand words could describe or express. All eyes were fixed on Jesus, hands filled with stones, an expectant, anticipatory hush waiting for his reply, because what could he possibly say to refute the justice and the rightness of this situation; according to Mosaic Law, surely this woman has to die?

Then Jesus says some words which bring an end to one kind of silence and introduce another; 'Let anyone among you who is without sin be the first to throw a stone at her,' and then he returns his finger to the sand. It is a brilliant manoeuvre which does not deny the Pharisees' right to present the adulterous woman for execution, it merely suggests that the sentence be carried out by those with the necessary credentials to do so. The silence now is not one of vengeful expectation, but instead soul searching introspection and self-examination, which leads those who would murder to one by one drop their stones and walk away. Gerard Manley Hopkins reflects thus:

'And thou art silent, whilst Thy world

Contends about its many creeds

And hosts confront with flags unfurled

And zeal is flushed and pity bleeds

And truth is heard, with tears impearled,

A moaning voice among the reeds.' [12]

Even though Jesus embraced silence throughout his ministry, it is also true that he was acutely aware of the dangers of suffering in silence. He encountered many people whose suffering had been a part of their lives since birth, and the Evangelists often tell us how long the afflicted had borne their diseases. If your illness or your long standing disability is of the kind that ostracises you from society, and causes others to regard you as dangerous or merely a figure for fun, then a common way to deal with it is to just acquiesce in your suffering. You accept the inevitability of your fate because nothing and no one is going to change, and the easier course is to stay mute, to suffer in silence. It was for good reason that Jesus rarely healed people privately but with his disciples or in front of a community, to which the restored person was often reunited after their healing encounter. The goal of the ten lepers being told to show the priests their newly acquired cleanliness, is that they would no longer be considered outcasts, untouchables, but be reintegrated back into society and reunited with the ones they loved.

We have seen the hidden, silent suffering of a woman, unseen and unnoticed in the Synagogue, who had been bent double in pain for eighteen long years. In the drawing out of her 'true colours' and her enduring in silent suffering, which we said we needed to recognise belongs to all of us, we forget, as with many others in the Gospels, one of the most obvious things about this healing. Jesus calls her to the front; he brings her into the public gaze so that others can see how much, and for how long, she has been suffering. A sacred society, with its rigid, unforgiving rules, has played its part to increase her suffering and has enforced the silent prison in which she found herself for so many years. Like the woman's twelve years of suffering from a haemorrhage, Jesus calls this woman a 'daughter', which is a reminder to all those around that they are part of the same family, damaged or not, and that when one suffers, everyone suffers together.

The part played by silence that we have identified in the Gospels becomes a lens into a terrible silence, which is at the heart of the crucifixion. The cross is the ultimate testimony to what it is to suffer in silence; from the abandonment by his friends in Gethsemane; to a cacophony of noise from the large crowd gathered outside Pilate's Praetorium making loud and insistent demands for Jesus' death; to the visceral taunting of Jesus by his accusers on the Via Dolorosa and on Golgotha's hill that did not stop until Jesus - after he had bewailed his

Father's silent absence during his greatest hour of need, in weak submission bowed his head and gave up his spirit. It recalls the silent suffering insulated in a hundred billion bottles washed up on the shore.

Anyone who is a practitioner of prayer and the Christian life knows what it's like to experience the absence of God in life. There appears to be a deafening silence in response to their prayers and a feeling that they are on their own in the darkness. It is a well attested and widely explored phenomenon that has exercised the minds and pens of theologians, mystics, and saints for centuries. Some of the greatest works of Christian literature have their basis in the enduring and understanding of this experience; R.S.Thomas describes God as:

> '..that great absence
>
> In our lives, the empty silence
>
> Within, the place where we go
>
> Seeking, not in hope to
>
> Arrive or find' [13]

The dreadful silence of the cross described in this way comes close to the experience of modern life alluded to earlier; that our ever increasing ability to communicate and to 'network' seems to have a curious, inverse relationship with the dread discovery, that more than ever we seem to live alone. We are prone to the dark and empty space of loneliness and an inability to maintain our various links between each other and to God.

Once, returning from a funeral, the undertaker asked me if I liked doing funerals. I said yes unequivocally; they are effective portals, not only to the transcendent, but for a unique opportunity and privilege, to come pastorally close to the bereaved, who are so often made vulnerable and defenceless by the impact of their loss. As the title of the song implies, there are different ways to perceive the presence of silence, and for those left to grieve the death of a loved one the ensuing 'silence' they experience in their lives can come to emulate the finality of death's silence. Those people whose lives have frozen in an attempt to recall and recreate a time of togetherness, remain clearly in my memory.

I remember visiting one woman a few months after the sudden death of her husband. The house had been turned into a museum, a frozen timepiece reflecting how things were the day before he died; including the newspaper draped over the arm of his favourite chair and his pyjamas still on the bed where he had left them. We sat together in complete silence until the sun went down and the house was enveloped in darkness, which was her cue to bid me farewell. Death is the greatest and most profound silence of all, yet it is the one experience, at some time or another, we share with Jesus Christ. He not only knew what it was to experience the loss of his beloved friend Lazarus - with a grief so deep that the Jews with him said to each other 'see how he loved him' - but who then had to endure the dreadful, imposing silence of the cross.

Nowhere is this more clearly demonstrated than at Golgotha. With the isolation that we've all felt when nobody seems to understand us; the terror we've all experienced when the misunderstanding of our needs, our purpose, our validity, and our identity is so comprehensive, that nothing we can say or do will alter another's opinion of us or why they think we are here. All we have is the anaemia of a silence, borne of a feeling of despair that nothing we have done or could ever do will make a difference.

The bystanders interpret Jesus' despairing cry from the cross as an appeal to Elijah to come and save him; they even get that wrong. After this moment, which seems to complete the silence of total isolation borne of hate and misunderstanding, there is nothing else left; just a loud cry after which Jesus breathes his last. All that remains now is the silence of death.

A Prophetic Silence...

It was stated earlier that one aspect of the revealing of our true colours by Christ's cross, was the necessity to realise that nothing can be hidden from God; and that our immense capacity to hate and to do harm lie exposed. Also that God's suffering and death draws us to a spectacle from which there is no escape, no hiding place. One aspect of the silence present at the cross is that which makes this judgement real, both on the perpetrators of evil and its original cause. For the woman caught in adultery, Jesus' silence in the face of the accusers about to stone her to death, is a foreshadowing of that silence present at death's darkest hour. The only thing standing between the woman and certain annihilation is Jesus' silence, charged as it is with the challenge to their conscience and the demand for a different kind of righteous justice. The dignity of slipping into silence of the Sinless One; he with the right credentials to execute justice, but who does so not by throwing stones, but by being thrown against the wood of the cross and executed with nails, is enough to send people away from the place of a skull, 'beating their breasts'. They are now convinced of their own unworthiness, just as those before who left the scene of stoning, one by one.

Jesus' silence before his accusers recalls that first confrontation in the wilderness, and, now as before, Satan's defeat is achieved not through the furious striving of one rival to subdue another, but in the quiet assurance that Jesus - the result of God's total emptying of himself and assuming the form of a servant - gives us the authentic human predisposition to doubt and despair; which confirms rather than denies his divinity and his status as Emmanuel - God with us. Here the silence of Jesus is the confidence of a victory that had been foretold through countless dreams and visions, to countless generations through endless cycles of sleepfulness and wakefulness, which was punctuated by the practice of prayer, the presence of God, and found its clearest expression in the wilderness and on the cross. Jesus' silence before Pilate's questions and his demand for answers, may well have been a deliberate ploy to cast himself as the Suffering Servant of Deutero-Isaiah who, 'Opened not his mouth; like a lamb that is led to the slaughter and like a sheep that before its shearers is dumb' [Isaiah 53:4]. It is possible to surmise Jesus' silence here though, as that of a serenity borne of a deep and wordless knowledge, fed by a vision planted in Christ's brain and nurtured in his heart. One that speaks of the inevitability of the cross not as the final stumbling block to hope, but as that painful and necessary vehicle that would ensure Satan's final defeat.

It is a serenity that only serves to inflame Pilate in his interrogation of Jesus and which ensures the exposure of his true colours, revealing his capacity for cruelty and murder. The earthly power with which Pilate threatens Jesus is no match for the real power implicit in Jesus' silence, which convicts and overcomes. Faced with him, whose silence betrays an assuredness of where all of this is leading and why, Pilate's own discomfort and uncertainty is put into sharp relief as he asks Jesus, 'What is truth?' The power of God's vision for the destiny of his world, conveyed in a vision softly creeping through countless individuals in many generations, and finally materialising in Jesus Christ is so powerful, that even Pilate's wife realises there is much more to this prisoner than meets the eye. 'Have nothing to do with that innocent man' she tells her husband, 'for today I have suffered a great deal because of a dream about him' [Matthew 27:19].

One of the most horrific aspects of the crucifixion is the fact that Jesus' mother had to witness it and for her, more than anyone attending that dreadful scene, we know that the beautiful baby and the vibrant young man she loved and cherished had become almost unrecognisable in his suffering. Isaiah tells us that, 'There were many who were astonished at him, so marred was his appearance, beyond human semblance'. The Psalmist tells us that God's suffering servant's complaint is that, 'I am poured out like water, and all my bones are out of joint....my mouth is dried up like a potsherd, and my tongue sticks to my jaws....my hands and feet have shrivelled; I can count all my bones' [Psalm 22:14].

The death of Jesus then, would have brought a final, blessed release from all his suffering, a silence ushered in by the bowing of his head and the giving up of his spirit, which speaks of intense relief. In St. John's Gospel, Jesus' last cry from the cross, 'It is finished', betrays a willingness and a permission to die because of a feeling of accomplishment that some kind of definitive 'end' has been reached. For Jesus' mother and the beloved disciple who witnessed first-hand the full horror of Golgotha, there must have also been a sense of release that the intolerable suffering of their loved one had finally come to an end; death's silence had finally replaced the travesty that passed for life on the cross. We know that for many who experience the aching loss of a cherished loved one, there is often a sense of release and a feeling of relief. Death, the final silence, has put an end to something which may have turned a beloved companion into a distant tormented stranger, and given an opportunity for those that are left to take stock and reshape their lives.

It is in the silence of the cross that the Church can trace its nativity. Jesus, in the moment of bowing his head and giving up his spirit, turned despair into hope for Mary and John who were standing near the foot of the cross. He offered, 'A hint that God after all has not abandoned his world, but has great plans for it', and ensuring that their suffering was no longer to be borne alone in silence. Precisely at the moment when Jesus finally acquiesces to death's call, redemption becomes a reality and certain death becomes a moment of transition and another chance to live for all of us.

Jesus' death is a chance for a woman who had been given a new son, and for a son who had been given a new mother, to reshape their lives together; a distant echo reverberating of an earlier occasion when another mother and son had been given to each other anew outside a town called Nain. It is noteworthy that Luke tells us that after the miracle of raising his son from the dead, 'Jesus gave him to his mother' [Luke 7: 11-15]. Here, in the gift of two people to each other at the foot of the cross, is the beginning of Christ's Church. For we know that in the days before Pentecost, the other disciples had gathered around Mary and John in an Upper Room in Jerusalem, 'constantly devoting themselves to prayer'[Acts 1: 12-14].

At silence's darkest heart flows blood and water from Jesus' pierced side, representing the two great sacraments of the Church. Those painful, love-filled fruits of the Kingdom that give us a taste of God that, 'teases us....but which one day will be ours....to have and to hold, to enjoy', and that, 'helps us to keep on trying to love because we know it's worth the cost'.

If it is right that the death of God is about a particular, awful silence that lies at the heart of the cross, and is one that enables us to perceive in the darkness and the stillness a hint that God has not abandoned his world after all, but has its future in mind, then at the moment of silence's most profound powerlessness there resides a powerful message that speaks of the promise of salvation. The words, 'It is finished', which usher in Jesus' death, also ushers in a new beginning. In the 'valley of the shadow of death', under a veil of tears

- where we seem to sit a lot of the time - here is something that seems to promise nothing but in fact delivers everything. Something, that in the eyes of the foolish seems to have died, but in fact, delivers hope that is full of immortality.

The testimony of the transforming presence of silence, manifested through the power of powerlessness and strength through weakness, has laid down a pattern of Christian experience and understanding that has stretched from the Desert Fathers to the present day. One modern, interesting example of this is referred to in the Simon and Garfunkel song, through the work of graffiti artists, who they call 'prophets'. These people are often unseen and unknown by the society their work seeks to address and are often despised by it, but their modern pictorial interpretation of life sometimes portrays uncomfortable truths which society finds very hard to name or to own. Currently one of the most famous (or is it infamous) is called Banksy.

As people pass between buildings, scurrying to and from their destinations, on the walls is graffiti which alerts them to what lies ahead. These are truths unspoken by those with no voice but whose messages, nevertheless, are powerfully displayed to people who talk without speaking; who hear without listening; who emulate the lack of vision causing Dylan's frustrated questioning in each line of 'Blowin' in the Wind'. It is a contemporary version of an ancient phenomenon; powerful truths pointed to by powerless people, the silence of their protests and warnings, noisily demanding attention and acceptance. Some of the most poignant graffiti appears on the very walls which have been built to inculcate fear and enforce exclusion, so that the walls themselves become signs and symbols of an eschatology which says that one day the evils they represent will be overthrown, and that one day truth, justice, and beauty will become a reality. [14]

The deep silence which is at the heart of the cross, though it seems to promise nothing more than the finality of Christ's death, is on the contrary a silence that is heavy with promise for all who, at one time or another, find themselves travelling along the difficult and painful Emmaus Road. It is a silence which has enormous importance for our pastoral care, the management of our grief at the loss of loved ones, and as a valid contribution to an understanding of the whole process of salvation.

To view the cross as the culmination of God's vision, his dream for the world, practised and rehearsed by the people he created is a reassurance to us. Whether we are asleep or awake, whether in the shopping centre or in the wilderness, there is nothing beyond His will and ability to use to speak to our hearts. The cross is like the ultimate piece of graffiti, it is a demonstration that Christian dreams can come true, and that divine vision can become reality. They may be born and live in silence, nobody may ever know the struggle we have to work at in prayer, to discover and to discern them. But Good Friday establishes that if silence is at the heart of the cross, then silence also puts the cross - that great testimony to the power of dreams and visions - at the heart of our lives.

IVOR MOODY
Songs for
the Soul
•
6

Let it Be

Discerning Direction

In May 1970, The Beatles released a song called 'Let It Be'. Its creator, Paul McCartney, pays tribute to the support he felt from his own mother, long since dead, who came to him in a dream at a time of much stress and anxiety. Her presence imparted a calmness and reassurance, and the inspiration to write the song.

It is a song which illustrates the bitter-sweet paradox between distance and closeness. Paul McCartney recognised immediately the religious connotations of the song. The words speak of a mother's watching presence; a comforter of the broken hearted people of the world, whose advice is to wait, to trust, and to believe that everything will come right in the end. Mary's wisdom is perceived at those times when loneliness and isolation, and the tendency to despair, have afflicted all of us.

I have placed, 'Let it Be', as the last song in the series because in writing about Mary, I came to realise that she embodies all the characteristics and qualities of the Christian journey which I have suggested are latent in the other songs. She is the one who both misunderstands and is misunderstood, but who eventually recognises truth. She is the one who - through her own magnificent true colours at the Incarnation and at the foot of the cross - finds strength and gives strength to others. But she also knows that because of the sword which had pierced her own soul, her prayers often seemed to be no more than the management of her loneliness; desperate messages in bottles. It is she who has come to stand for justice and equality, enabling others to encounter reconciliation and a vision of the heavenly shore, but it is the discovery of a power borne not through action, but through silence and stillness.

Above all, Mary is another in the long line of those vulnerable, unlikely people that have been traced through this book - Moses, David, Jeremiah and many others - who God chooses and calls to influence the world. Perhaps, through her vocation, we can discern most clearly the direction God calls us to follow in our own lives, she whose life is intimately intertwined with her divine son, and who is transformed from a shy virgin mother to a leader and inspirer of the earliest church.

Like the other songs referred to in this book, here is some secular poetry that started out with no overt religious meaning or purpose, but nevertheless, reveals a latent spiritual potential; pearls of great value for Christians as they journey, struggling to make sense of their faith in a postmodern world.

Throughout my ministry, the recognition and veneration of the Virgin Mary - the inclusion of her within mainstream Christian teaching, preaching, and worship - has been a thorn in the side of many Christians and Christian communities. For many, any identification of her divine status detracts from the honouring of Jesus Christ as the only path to salvation. I have been surprised and saddened, not only by the hostility and distrust towards any kind of recognition of Mary's importance and place within salvation's story, but how impoverished people's understanding of their faith has been as a result. If, as Christianity has always held to be true, that it is in Jesus Christ alone that our lives are sustained and find meaning, then the person who was his mother and gave him life cannot help but be a central theme of Christian reflection.

The various 'sightings' of Mary during the last two hundred years or so in places like Lourdes, Fatima, and elsewhere - which remain hugely important places of pilgrimage - suggest that the presence of the Virgin Mary breaking into human life is a phenomenon that refuses to be silenced. For the vast majority of these appearances, it was those who were without status or power that first saw them and reported them. For example, the Marian Shrine at Guadeloupe was created as a result of a beautiful young woman appearing to a young peasant named Juan Diego on a road outside the city. She told him of her desire for a church to be built in that place, which would become a refuge for all the poor and downtrodden of the land. The shrine at Lourdes was the result of the appearance of a 'small young lady' clothed in white to Bernadette Soubirous, a fourteen year old girl. After several visions she was told that a chapel should be built in the grotto, which was near a rubbish dump, where she had first seen the young woman. Both of these appearances were to people of no account or influence, and occurred in areas far removed from centres of wealth and power.

Despite the scepticism with which many greet these stories, scripture is clear that a spiritual experience of Mary in a person's life has its basis in something that happened to Mary herself. This can describe and define the experience of so many people who become aware of God's desire to be in a relationship with them - the discernment of a 'vocation' that speaks of a purpose and a direction to our Christian faith. This is a relationship whose beginning I can still accurately and precisely recall, that planted within me a feeling that things would never be the same again. I was on a coach, travelling up the M1 motorway to see family after Christmas, and I was reading a book called 'God's Smuggler' by Brother Andrew. He was a Dutch mercenary who became a Christian and his story suddenly and very powerfully changed my own. There were no bright lights or dramatic visionary experiences but nevertheless, the M1 became my 'Damascus Road'. My eyes were opened and I arrived at my destination far different from when I had started.

Wisdom's Words

Mary was someone who could trace her vocation to a specific point and place in time, and whose relationship with her son could be traced to the point in her life when her existence would be changed forever. A young girl facing insurmountable poverty, scratching out a subsistence living in an obscure, nowhere community. She suddenly becomes aware that life is no longer the two-dimensional entity she thought it to be, but was instead interesting and significant for the unfolding of the divine plan of salvation for mankind. Luke tells us:

> 'In the sixth month the Angel Gabriel was sent by God to a town in Galilee called Nazareth, to a virgin engaged to a man whose name was Joseph, of the House of David. The Virgin's name was Mary'. [Luke 1: 26-27]

This verse is important for its preciseness, the way it identifies names in the establishment of our identities, and the significance of God's intersection of our lives. We are told many things when this event happened, who the messenger was, where the message was delivered, the status of the person who received that message, the name of the person's husband to be, the location of his Jewish heritage, and the identity of the person that had been singled out to receive the message.

It is one of the most powerful and significant verses in the whole of scripture. A moment when thousands of years of God's dealings with his Chosen People, and by association other nations of the world, funnels down into the overshadowing of a virgin by the power of the Most High and the birth of He who would be called holy - the Son of God. Her experience gives us a common and shared identity, because we find all of our vocations in hers. She becomes another one in that great company of women and men of faith. This was an event, dreamed of by many prophets and kings, whose own spiritual experience of call and vocation was an inspiration for Jesus' own sense of purpose and direction. It is also reflective of, 'The power of God's vision for the destiny of his world, conveyed in a vision softly creeping through numberless individuals in many generations and finally materialising in Jesus Christ'.

Gabriel's first words to Mary are, 'Greetings favoured one! The Lord is with you'. God's favour is more than just being singled out for a job because she was considered strong enough and faithful enough to carry out God's plans, even in the company of many prophets who preceded her, her true colours were known and treasured by God before she was formed in the womb. In her 'favouring' there is a richness to her vocation, which can help us understand how we might fulfil the purpose of God in our lives, despite a despondency that our Christian faith might ever make a difference; and despite prayers which are so often flung against the sky in an attempt to attract the attention of a God conspicuous by his absence.

The Incarnation means nothing less than the giving of Mary's own substance to the Christ Child and to not grasp that, is to not fully understand the impact of God's self-emptying described by Paul, which was mentioned earlier. Like all children, Jesus would have inherited some of her features. A unique, umbilical cord link to that piece of the material world, with his first experience of food, emotions, and language donated by his mother Mary.

Mary endured a difficult and dangerous journey to Bethlehem, only to deliver Jesus in a stable. She wrapped him up in swaddling cloths and laid him in a manger; she provided him with food and warmth in the midst of the cold, unforgiving surroundings. Although the Word had become flesh, because of the Incarnation, he would have to learn the art of language all over again; and it was Mary who was the one required to educate the Word to learn words.

A lot of Christian art, especially iconography, stylises the relationship between the Virgin Mother and her beloved child. A common portrayal, in one way or another, is a serene Jesus sitting on the lap of his equally serene mother facing forwards, engaging in eye contact with those who are looking upon the mother and child. Though surely, he would have been like any other child on his mother's lap; eager to get as close as possible to the familiar, comforting contours of his mother's body, facing inwards to get as close as he could to the maternal cheek, wriggling and squirming to make sure he is as secure as he possibly can be in the arms of the one who brought him to life. The image of a child who cannot bear to be separated from his mother can dramatically portray God's delight in humanity, not because he is needful of anything we might give to him, but because he recognises with joy who Mary is, and how, from now on, God can 'inhabit' his creation like never before. In a passionate plea for deliverance from suffering and hostility, in a psalm which links us directly with Jesus' experience on Good Friday, the Psalmist reflects back on a time of safety and comfort when as a child, like the infant Christ on his mother's lap, God's maternal presence provided shelter and protection from a hostile world.

> "Yet it was you who took me from the womb; you kept me safe on my mother's breast. On you I was cast from my birth, and since my mother bore me you have been my God. Do not be far from me, for trouble is near and there is no one to help." [Psalm 22:9-11]

This loving communication throws further light on some of the Gospel stories studied so far in this narrative. In the story of the widow of Nain, Luke communicates Jesus' compassion for this woman's plight, a widow he says had lost her only son. In a child's excitement to get as close to his mother's cheek as he can, Jesus would have known, in the depths of his heart, what the tragic experience of loss might feel like for a mother who would have memories of a wriggling, squirming child on her lap, anxious to drink in her love. The Son, who from the cross gave his mother into the care of his greatest friend, already knew how human company, interaction, and the need to embrace and be embraced is essential to our lives. Just as the father of the prodigal son watches and waits for his younger son's return and then throws his arms around his neck when they are finally reunited.

In the story of the raising of Jairus' daughter, Mark and Luke recount that Jesus asked her parents to go into the room with him. Rescued from the sleep of death, the little girl's newly opened eyes would have fallen upon her parents, the first to witness the little girl returning to life and who, after their daughter's frightening experience, would now welcome her back to comfort, to security, and to familiarity. Mark also tells us that Jesus, 'Told them to give her something to eat'. I am sure this was not merely an instruction to help the little girl, who no doubt had been made weak as a result of her illness, it was also to reunite the family through that thoroughly human activity of sharing food. After the healing, there is also a restoration with those who most loved her and the miracle is not complete without it. [Mark 5:35-43]

When a father begs Jesus to heal his demon possessed son, the casting out is so difficult and so violent that the onlookers assume that the boy has died. However, Mark tells us that Jesus, 'took him by the hand and lifted him up, and he was able to stand'. It is Luke alone who gives us the next bit of precious information, 'Jesus rebuked the unclean spirit, healed the boy and gave him back to his father.' [Luke 9:37-43] This bond of love between parent and child indelibly colours Jesus' perception of people and their needs. It also has implications for the core of Jesus' message, because the affection first intimately shared between Mary and Jesus and taught to him from parents that settled with him in Nazareth and to whom he was obedient, became the benchmark for Jesus' love and care for others, and the message to us that we need to do the same.

In Darkness' Hour

The source of Jesus' agony in the Garden of Gethsemane is the knowledge that the Kingdom of God can only be established if a sword pierces his own heart. The words, 'not my will but yours be done', are words echoed by his mother's own to the angel at the Annunciation, 'Here am I, the servant of the Lord; let it be with me according to your word'. 'Your will be done', is a servant language used by the mother, who through her life and example, teaches her son the same response. Jesus' words, spoken from the cross, 'Father forgive them, for they do not know what they are doing' are pre-empted by Mary, who had to live them and endure them first. Her own 'stature of waiting' reveals how one of the most effective tools to help ensure the continuance of the Good News is something that lies within grasp of us all - to forgive those who would trespass against us.

The cruel mistreatment and destruction of her precious son, whom she had fed, nurtured, taught, and loved, is one of the greatest scandals of the cross. The agony borne of a silence generated by an incapability to change the situation is replicated today, thousands of times every day, in the silent witness of those who are compelled to watch a cruel, merciless pageant unfold involving the ones they love. We are all too familiar with parents who are forced to bear the violent loss of their children, and considering the unimaginable anger and grief spawned, it is not surprising that the media often report the extraordinary statements of forgiveness that are sometimes given to those who have committed the murder of their loved ones. The image of Mary standing at the foot of the cross having to forgive so many who, in so many different ways, contributed to her son's death is a pattern for all of those later reconciliations.

This bond between mother and son is not illustrated or reported in the Gospels, rather the opposite is depicted. Apart from the Christmas and Easter stories, Mary makes three appearances in the course of Jesus' ministry. Each of these times it is only to acquiesce to her son's authority and mission. The first has already been seen, in an angry exchange with her twelve year old son in the Temple, when a mother's deep relief at finding her missing son after three days' search clashes with his assertion that, because of who and what he is, he is exactly where he should be. At a wedding in Cana in Galilee, where Jesus and his family are guests, a mother's inclination to tell her son that the celebrations are in danger of collapse because the wine has run out is met with cold disinterest; 'Woman, what concern is that to you and to me? My hour has not yet come' [John 2:1-12]. When Mary and the family come looking for Jesus and he is told they are waiting for him, he glances at the crowd gathered around him, hanging on his every word, and describes his family as *anyone* who does the will of God. [Mark 3:31-35]

Jesus frequently addresses Mary with the anonymous term 'woman'. It has been argued that this title is a preparation by Jesus of the nature and status that Mary will have in the infant church. That his encounters with her are 'training grounds' for her to learn the true meaning of his identity and his mission, so that at the cross the 'Woman' who is given to John is no longer simply his mother, but has become the mother of all the disciples and the Christian community. Luke is careful to tell us that at the very beginning of their Christian witness, the disciples and Jesus' other closest companions are at prayer with Jesus' mother.

However, this type of appraisal of the encounters between Jesus and his mother, misses something very important about the meaning of Mary for those in the Church today. Elsewhere in the Gospels when Jesus uses the mode of address 'woman', it is usually a title that precedes and paves the way for a much warmer rapprochement between Jesus and the female. Earlier we came across the story of a woman in the Synagogue, hunched over after eighteen years of pain. Her healing begins with Jesus saying, 'Woman, you are set free from your ailment'. The urgency for this woman's well-being after suffering for so long, stirs within him a compassionate zeal for the task. The 'woman' now becomes a 'Daughter of Abraham', one whose status, as well as her long endurance of pain, demands that she be released from her bondage.

It is this same longevity of suffering that melts Jesus' heart when the woman, who had suffered for twelve years from haemorrhaging, is called out from her anonymity in the crowd pressing around Jesus and granted the status of 'Daughter'; who could then go in peace because her faith had made her well. In the Easter Garden, Mary Magdalene is also addressed as 'woman', both by the angels who sat at the head and feet where the body of Jesus had lain, and by a man she had assumed was the gardener. Her distress at not finding the body of Jesus is plain to see and the one thing that transforms that anguish into joy is a reconfiguring of her identity. The gardener calls her by her name, and Jesus' identification of her is reciprocated. She addresses him as 'Rabbouni' - teacher - a term of affection that marks him as her Saviour and her friend. It was a term of endearment used by Jesus' closest companions; when Martha goes to Mary and tells her that Jesus, on his way to Lazarus' tomb, is enquiring after her she says, 'The Teacher is here and is calling for you' [John 11:17-28; 20:11-18].

In all of the encounters reported in the Gospels between Jesus and his mother, we are never told of a similar kind of warm relationship or reunion between them. Even though there will be comfort for her grief at the foot of the cross, when she is given to John, even though the 'gift' of the Mother of God and the Beloved Disciple to each other 'is a moment of transition and a moving on for them both', and is of enormous significance for the birth of the Christian Church, Mary nevertheless remains, 'Woman'.

Her silence in the Gospels refers to something we have all had to cope with in our lives; trying to relate to a God who so often appears cold, distant, and elusive. The sword which pierced Mary's heart was not just the loss of her first born son, nor was it the gradual realisation of his mission and destiny, but it was the requirement for her to understand and to accept his *distance* from her. She stands alongside us in our common experience of God's elusiveness, her lament being:

"I opened to my beloved, but my beloved had turned and was gone. My soul failed me when he spoke. I sought him, but did not find him; I called him, but he gave no answer." [Song of Solomon 5:6]

This experience speaks powerfully to our own strivings, identified by R.S. Thomas, to understand and to accept the oft-repeated experience of trying to say our prayers to come close to God, only to find that, 'great absence in our lives, the empty silence within'.

The retort by their twelve year old son, that Mary and Joseph should have known that he would have been in the Temple conversing with the scribes and the doctors of the law, brings Mary to a realisation of who and what he really was, and therefore to a loneliness of *difference*. What begins as a typical family encounter, transforms into a statement that betrays Jesus' true parentage, and pushes his mother into a mode of silent acceptance. Mary's rebuke to her twelve year old son in the Temple, 'Child, why have you treated us like this? Look, your father and I have been searching for you in great anxiety', is the repeated cry of all Christian experience at one time or another.

Even though the handing over of mother to disciple and disciple to mother represents the centre around which the infant church was to gather, the church's discipleship and mission locates itself primarily in the silent heart of Mary. She who had to struggle with the same silence and elusiveness of God as we do; and the culmination of that distance between the Son and his mother, lies in Mary witnessing her own son's death.

In a book called 'Mary Shadow of Grace', Megan McKenna argues that the giving of Mary to the Beloved Disciple John, is indicative of Mary being gifted as a mother to all the disciples and to the whole family of God. It is evidence that in death, the mother/son relationship ceases to be relevant. However, the connection present between mother and son at the cross was as strong and life giving as the physical one that would have been severed at birth, highlighted by St. John who tells us that, 'Jesus saw his mother, and the disciple whom he loved standing beside her'. Their proximity to the cross meant that they were close enough to hear him commit them into each other's care. Even though Mary was used to treasuring and keeping in her heart all that she witnessed and all that was being said about him, her silent, watching presence by the cross is all the more powerful. It is a demonstration that her filial and prayerful support for her son was absolute, and took her to the heart of darkness; because she ended up there, we can be confident she was everywhere where Jesus was, her silence meaning not disinterest or disconnectedness, but a passionate belief and support for who he was and what he stood for.

As Mary stands by the cross, there is a bond of love between mother and Son which defies description, and through the cross it has become a bond which is possible for all of us. Much of the time it seems to lie beyond the grasp of our experience, but it underpins all of our relationships with and our questionings about God and our faith; it is the thing that keeps us flinging our prayers skyward.

Mary never gives up on her son. Despite experiencing a directly proportionate relationship between Jesus' growing up and growing away to be a light for revelation to the Gentiles, and the sword thrust into her faithful Jewish soul, there is something beyond an utter belief in his cause. Something even beyond a vision of a redeemed, hope-filled future that could not be obliterated by the agony of Good Friday, which brought her into close proximity with her son's crucified body. It was her experience of being the first one to love Christ and the first to be loved by him, which transcends all else; even the pain and agony of watching her son die; even the pain of having to endure so much elusiveness from God. It is no mistake that Mary is often addressed as 'Our Lady', because it is the experience of so many that, in one way or another, Mary comes to them with her wisdom and counsel. So that should indicate to us that Mary needs to be a central figure in our prayer and our spirituality.

An Answer Awaits

One of the things that helped to keep Mary at the foot of the cross was a belief that the events of Good Friday belonged to a history that also promised a future. In the expression of her Magnificat at the beginning of Luke's Gospel, Mary places the birth of God's Son within a historical and liturgical frame-work, and therefore gives context and meaning to when she says 'yes' to God that it may be to her, according to his word. This song of praise to God is a testimony to His favouring of the poor and faithfulness towards his people. He has, 'Helped Israel...according to the promise he made to our ancestors', all of this demonstrates not only the belonging and identity of Mary, but also that of her unborn son [Luke 1:46-55].

The power of Mary's Magnificat derives not only from what it says, but the context in which it is spoken. Mary does what many of us would when faced with such a shattering experience that we simply cannot take it in, she goes to visit someone who might understand and sympathise with her, because this person too has endured a miraculous, earth shattering event of her own. She finds solace and meaning from her cousin Elizabeth, who was family, part of that same generational context into which their sons were also going to be born. It is out of *that* context - of ancestry, of membership, of a deep affinity with His chosen but oppressed people - that the comprehension of God's purposes come to fruition. Michael O'Siadhail describes it as a:

'Lineage of love, strange dynasty
    beyond the blood, every succession
wills on the gift; a current
    skips from fingertip to tip
along life-giving lines, as once,
    suddenly, thumbing through a treasury
we find ourselves stumble on
    forerunners who forefather us....' [15]

Now a chain reaction has been set in place. When in Elizabeth's womb, the future John the Baptist realises he is in the presence of the Christ Child, and leaps for joy. He knows that the salvation of the world is near, which up to that point had been hidden from Elizabeth, for whom the true miracle of her pregnancy is the solution to her childlessness. Yet the presence of Jesus creating the reaction that it did in her own child, suddenly opens Elizabeth's eyes and she realises that something greater than an end to her childlessness is here. Her reaction in turn opens Mary's eyes and in the words of the Magnificat, which Mary then speaks, all the fear and questioning she has experienced in front of Gabriel - about what sort of greeting this might mean and the apparent impossibility of her having fallen pregnant in the first place - finds its true meaning and direction. For now God, 'Has looked with favour on the lowliness of his servant...for the Mighty One has done great things for me'. Finding meaning in her own situation, experience in the remote hill country of a land that she loved and for which she had a fierce sense of belonging, and amongst family and friends who surrounded her and supported her, then she is able to see that what has happened has truly global significance. Not only is, 'His mercy....for those who fear him from generation to generation', but for Mary, those same generations will forever call her blessed.

All of this was to find its physical manifestation and full significance on that fateful day in the Synagogue at Nazareth, the day when Jesus begins his public ministry. Mary's task of raising Jesus reinforces her sense of belonging and identity amongst those who shared her life. We can never know how *normal* life was for this poor Jewish couple from an obscure little town, trying to bring up a child who was special beyond words. Nor will we know quite how successfully they, as the Holy Family, had integrated into that community, though Luke tells us that on a particular Sabbath, Jesus went to the Synagogue, 'as was his custom'. Mary and Joseph tried to make him feel like a part of the community, which surrounded him by immersing him in the liturgical, worshipping life of his people, that had a long story of suffering, pilgrimage, disaster, and promise. Jesus was obviously no stranger to this as the Synagogue attendant gave him the honour of reading from the sacred scrolls that day.

The incredulous and scandalised reactions to Jesus' interpretation of the prophet's words he had just read out - that he was the fulfilment of Isaiah's prophecy - centred on the misunderstanding of who Jesus actually was. The furious congregation in the Synagogue that morning, who thought that Jesus was making absurd, outrageous claims about himself, also based those accusations on the premise of his and his family's familiarity to them. We know who this man is and to whom he belongs they say, and for that reason, what he is saying is not only blasphemy, it is nonsense.

The redemptive process initiated by Christ's cross is reflected by Mary's maternal presence which now stands by her suffering Son. Through her silent grief and watching she emulates what he will do for all people for all time; to proclaim liberty to captives, recovery of sight to the blind, and let the oppressed go free. It is also a signal for the church to come from she who had become the mother of all the disciples,which will define the behaviour and outlook of the whole Christian community. A woman who deeply understands the importance of history and community - who is present at the cross with her sister (the wife of Clopas), and Mary Magdalene, and who is given to the beloved disciple - lends credence and worth to the concept that this loving exchange is symbolic of the community of the church, of the handing on of each of us to the other, and which begins then and there.

Because Mary was able to accept and not reject the intervention of God into his world, to understand it and contextualise it as a continuation rather than as a disruption of history, then the event of the crucifixion becomes part of a much larger picture, where ultimately there is hope rather than despair. Therein lies Mary's gift to all who seek to live in Christian community, but who often despair of its muddled, painful history, and its continuation amidst a scornful, self-regarding world, and its ability to change and transform that global community.

In this context, it is significant that in the song 'Let it Be', Mary's wisdom is perceived at precisely those times when loneliness and isolation, and the tendency to despair and be overwhelmed have afflicted us all - in times of trouble, in the hour of darkness, when the night is cloudy. The comfort she brings to us is a wisdom that says it is still possible to make deep connections in the midst of life's puzzling complexities; it is still possible to acknowledge that human community - despite all its futile, pain-filled endeavour - can be a tremendous gift and a reality check for those in danger of losing hope.

Jesus' teachings and actions, foreshadowed by his mother, sent him to the cross in a fit of jealousy and rage by those who were threatened by his counter cultural message that was poised to forever upset the status quo. We may believe the cross to be the ultimate sign of God's victory, fixed in an eternal posture of embrace, but Christ's violent death and the sheer bloodiness of the cross, ensured that Mary's vision lived out and made possible by her son, was yet to be fully realised. Love's supremacy is set within the continuing experience of pain; in us the drama of divine purpose continues its unfolding but it does so within a Christianity, which experiences at its centre the constant juggling of love and pain.

Consequently, Mary has been at the forefront of one of the most phenomenal movements to sweep through the church since the 1960's, called Liberation Theology. Although its roots are in Latin America, it is a global phenomena with its focus on the interface between the Christian faith and the sufferings and struggles of the poor, and a theological critique of society, the church, and Christianity. One of the dangers with downplaying or sidestepping Mary's importance and influence in the Christian tradition, is to see her simply as a comforter of the afflicted. However, the fact is Mary's Magnificat declaration has identified her with the struggle of the poor, and has made her a powerful ally in Liberation Theology's quest to overturn unjust structures, and to identify the tasks and responsibilities of a church which must have a bias to the poor. This has led to Mary being seen not only as a companion in suffering, but as a challenger to those who are complicit in that suffering.

The aloofness between mother and son highlighted earlier, has important things to say about how Mary stands alongside us in the same shared struggle to make sense of

God's often elusiveness in our lives and our prayers. If the Magnificat is interpreted as a gauntlet thrown down to the church to stand alongside God's downtrodden people, then Mary's silence and distance takes on a new and exciting meaning. Now her silence becomes powerful, and her gentle, unassuming appearances in the Gospels become graffiti-like. The words of the Magnificat testifies to powerful truths which powerless people are able to point to, 'whose messages...are powerfully displayed to people who talk without speaking, who hear without listening'. Not only Mary's words, but her actions become a language which is liberated, defiant, anticipatory, and that draws its legitimacy not from the current context, but from the future vision of God's Kingdom; when mourning and crying will be no more.

From a celebration of Mary's motherhood that influenced so much of Jesus' own personality and ministry; to a positive acceptance of Mary's loneliness who remains 'woman' despite her attentiveness to Jesus; to a recognition of her son's destiny through her own grasp of history and through God's relationship with his people which gives us all hope of understanding the perplexing events that surrounds us. We are now at a threshold of understanding something of her significance to us and the church, not despite her wilderness presence in the Gospels but because of it.

We can draw comfort from Mary's graffiti-like silence, because what helps to bind us together as a community of Christians, is the continuing task of liberation for all of God's people; which was first proclaimed by Mary in her Magnificat and lived out at the foot of the cross. It speaks of a witness that we all share by virtue of our own closeness to Jesus' cross. That here is salvation's 'unfinished business', and that Mary's future is all of ours in a church called to continue the task of filling the hungry with good things.

If it is true that one of the main things keeping Mary at the foot of the cross was her wisdom that her son's crucifixion *made sense*, that history had predicted it and the future would forever be affected by it, then this wasn't merely an intellectual reaction, it was an emotional one. In the midst of so much loss, grief, and anxiety, engendered by Gabriel's message, the Magnificat comes almost as a 'bolt out of the blue'. It is a sudden, impassioned, triumphant outpouring of joy triggered by a moment of revelation from a cousin, herself struggling to understand what is happening, and it gives us all a glimpse of heaven right in the midst of the two-dimensional uncertainty and struggle which seems to pass as life most of the time.

These are moments when, like Mary, our vocations are centred by a touch of God's finger; eternity breaks into time and time is taken up into eternity. In the tension between the now and the not yet, in the relationship between closeness and distance, here is the glimpse of glory highlighted earlier, 'that tantalises us, that disappears around the corner just as our eyes focus, that teases us like a God who hides in a burning bush, or speaks in a still small voice, but which one day will be ours fully to possess'. This is revealed in the Eucharist and now shown forth in the faithful, persevering lives of all her children; which gives us the ultimate cause for hope that one day our liberation will be a reality.

Let it Be

Notes

(All scriptural quotations are taken from the Holy Bible New Revised Standard Version NRSV).

1. Andrew Walker, *Telling the Story* (London: SPCK, 1996), p.99

2. Ivor Moody, *Did not our hearts burn within us? Uncovering a Sacred Language for a Secular University*: dissertation for an MA in Pastoral Theology with the Cambridge Theological Federation (Anglia Polytechnic University, 2003), p.14

3. Miroslav Volf, *Exclusion and Embrace* (Nashville: Abingdon Press, 1996.)

4. Malcolm Guite, *A New Start* (Chelmsford: Anglia Ruskin University, 2000), pp.6-7. This publication was the result of a request to the Chaplaincy from Anglia Ruskin University that it helped the institution to mark the centenary in some significant way. Malcolm and I decided to celebrate what we considered the University did best; to encourage and walk alongside students, many of them in later life and many who had missed out on education the first time round, either through circumstance, disability, or often because the 'system' had convinced them that University was beyond their reach. Students who in many cases had to study, and who completed their degrees, in the face of huge personal challenges and adversity, and how their struggle to survive and to achieve at University represented a new start for them all. Malcolm writes, *"Something was at work in all these students' lives. Something which refused to accept the ultimacy of failure. Something which kept them going. Something which took them through their 'Good Friday' and brought them to a new beginning."* (p.7.)

5. In an absorbing and important book by Diane Purkiss called *The English Civil War* (London: Harper Collins, 2006), she approaches the war from a sociological perspective, looking at the lives, beliefs, and practices of various individuals from across the social spectrum and on both sides of the political and ideological divide. She does so not only to point up the English Civil War as one of the most important events in our history and a prime catalyst in the shaping of modern society (and an event which still suffers lamentable neglect on schools historical curricula), but because the ordinary people who fought in this war are our lineal descendants, and our contemporary stories of suffering and conflict, religious, political, personal, find meaning and context in theirs.

6. Mark 15:39. Matthew has the same declaration by the centurion, but Mark has a unique and very important little detail; he tells us that the centurion 'stood facing him' (Jesus), more than that merely the centurion was 'with' Jesus. Mark's specific placing of the centurion directly in front of the cross implies that this soldier would not have missed the final words of Jesus and the moment when he breathed his last, and so, gazing directly onto the crucified form, his declaration in Mark's Gospel is especially significant and infused with meaning.

7. C.S. Lewis, *A Grief Observed* from (London: Faber & Faber Ltd, 2013), pp.13-14. The title of this quote was one spoken by his wife Joy when trying to describe what her impending death felt like.

8. R.S. Thomas, *Folk Tale* from *Collected Poems 1945-1990* (London: Phoenix, 2000), p.517

9. George Herbert, *Love* in *Poem for the Day* ed. Nicholas Albery (London: Chatto & Windus, 2001), p.70

10. Volf, *Exclusion and Embrace* pp.135-136

11. Walter Brueggemann, *Cadences of Home; Preaching among Exiles* (Kentucky: Westminster John Knox Press, 1997). Writing from within what he calls a 'White European story' and focussed particularly on the imposition of the American way of life and the American dream, Brueggemann argues that faith communities find themselves in a situation of exile which bears some comparison with the ancient Israelites and their Babylonian captivity. In the face of a dominant, hegemonic, powerful narrative driven by success, prosperity and security, and an all-pervasive secularism, there is a Western narrative, perhaps reflected and fuelled by the anti-terrorist warlike rhetoric that pervades politics and the media, that now has a tendency to push to the margins issues of justice and inclusion; consequently there is a counter cultural language which the faith communities need to reacquire and reinvest with credibility and substance.

12. Gerard Manley Hopkins, *Nondum* in *The Poems of Gerard Manley Hopkins* eds. W.H. Gardner & N.H. Mackenzie (London: Oxford University Press, 1967), pp.32-33

13. R.S. Thomas, *Via Negativa* in *Collected Poems 1945-1990,* p.220

14. Two notable examples are the Berlin and Palestinian walls, both built with the specific intention to intimidate and divide. The Palestinian wall still stands, and Banksy's art which adorns it reminds us that the human yearning for freedom and the existence of beauty remain resolute; just above and beyond the grey forbidding structure that would seem to deny the possibility of either. To visit the remnants of the Berlin wall is to witness the ef-

ficacy and power of the messages of numerous prophets whose defiant words and images of peace, love, and reunion finally seemed to come to pass when the wall was torn down in 1989. An internet search easily reveals hundreds of powerful graffiti images that describe and define these two monuments to the dreadful consequences of human hate and misunderstanding.

15. Micheal O'Siadhail, *Homage* in *Micheal O'Siadhail Poems 1975-1995* (Newcastle Upon Tyne: Bloodaxe Books Ltd, 1999), p.73

WAKING UP